Leaf Leap

On brightly-colored paper, reproduce the leaf pattern on page 4. Make 10 copies. Tape copies securely to the floor, in a staggered pattern, a small leap apart. With a bold marker, number the leaves from 1-10. Have children leap from leaf to leaf, in numerical order. They can also leap from 10-1 or to even or odd numbers.

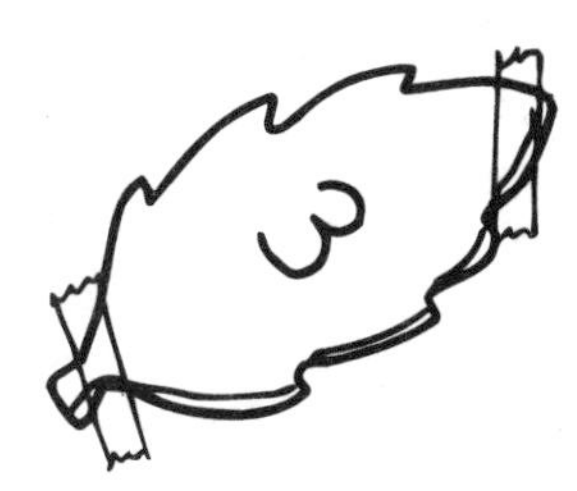

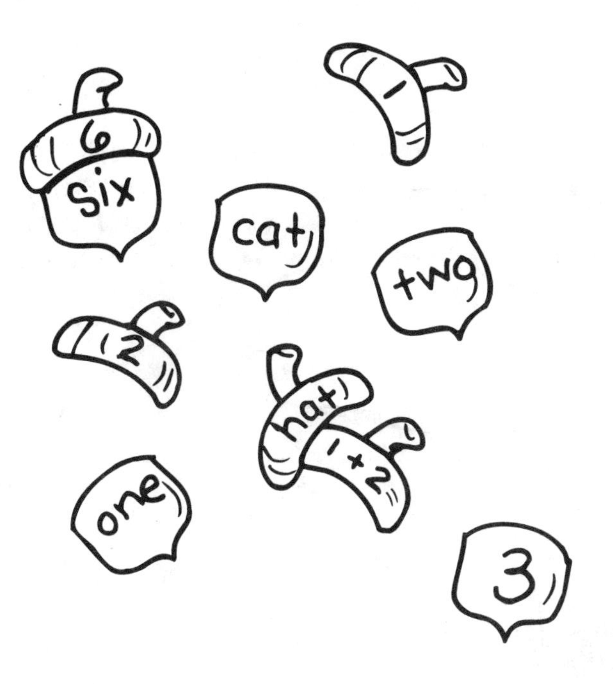

Acorn Match

Reproduce the acorn patterns provided on page 4. With a black marker, write matching facts on each half, such as "6" and "six" or "1 + 2 =" and "3" or rhyming words. Mix the halves and have children make matches. Then glue the acorns to colored paper.

Harvest Words

Reproduce several copies of each of the produce patterns on page 5 on brightly colored paper. Cut the patterns out. On each fruit or vegetable, have children write one word to describe it. Glue the "harvest" to a paper plate and use as inspiration for a class writing project.

Activity Patterns

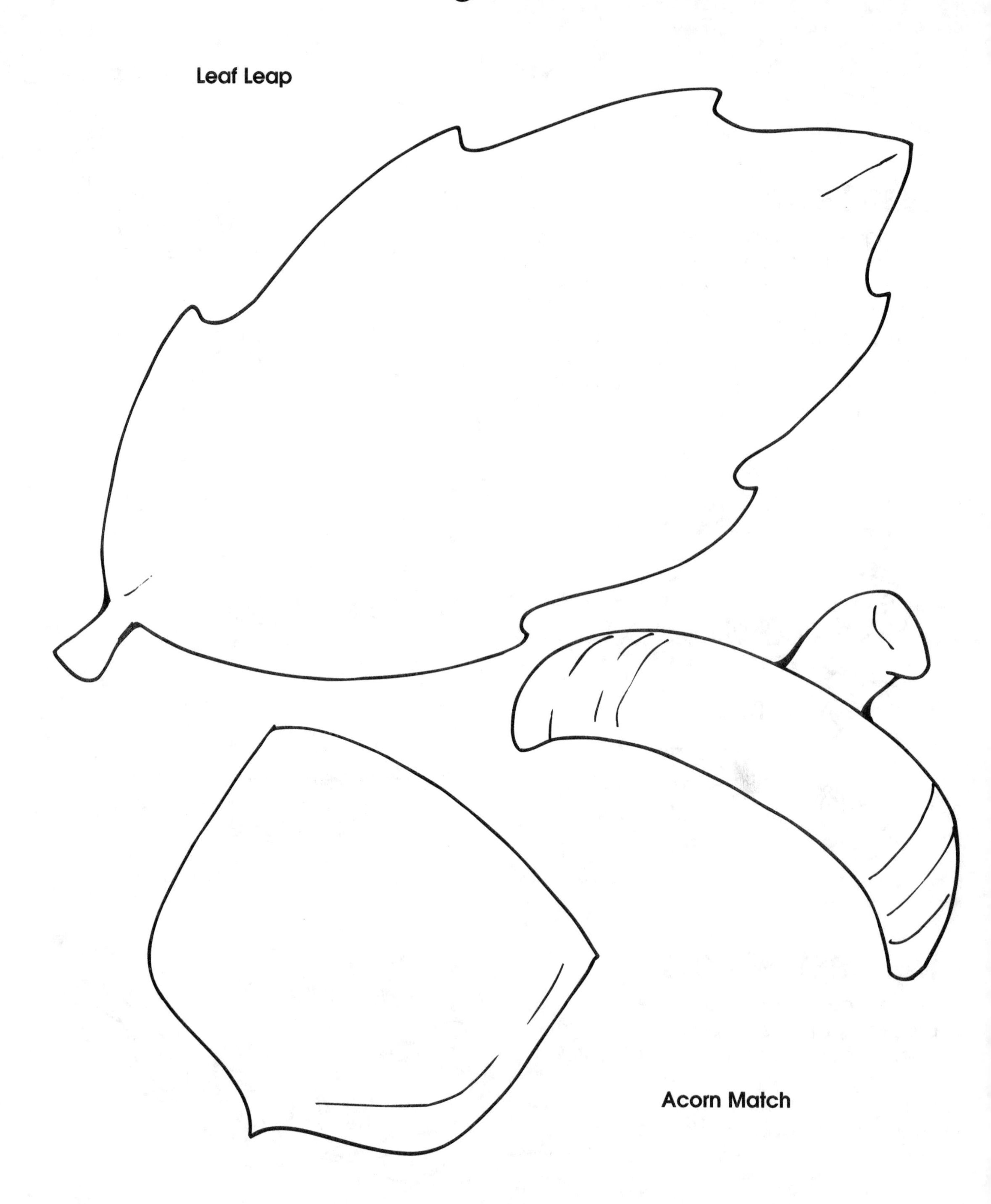

Activity Patterns

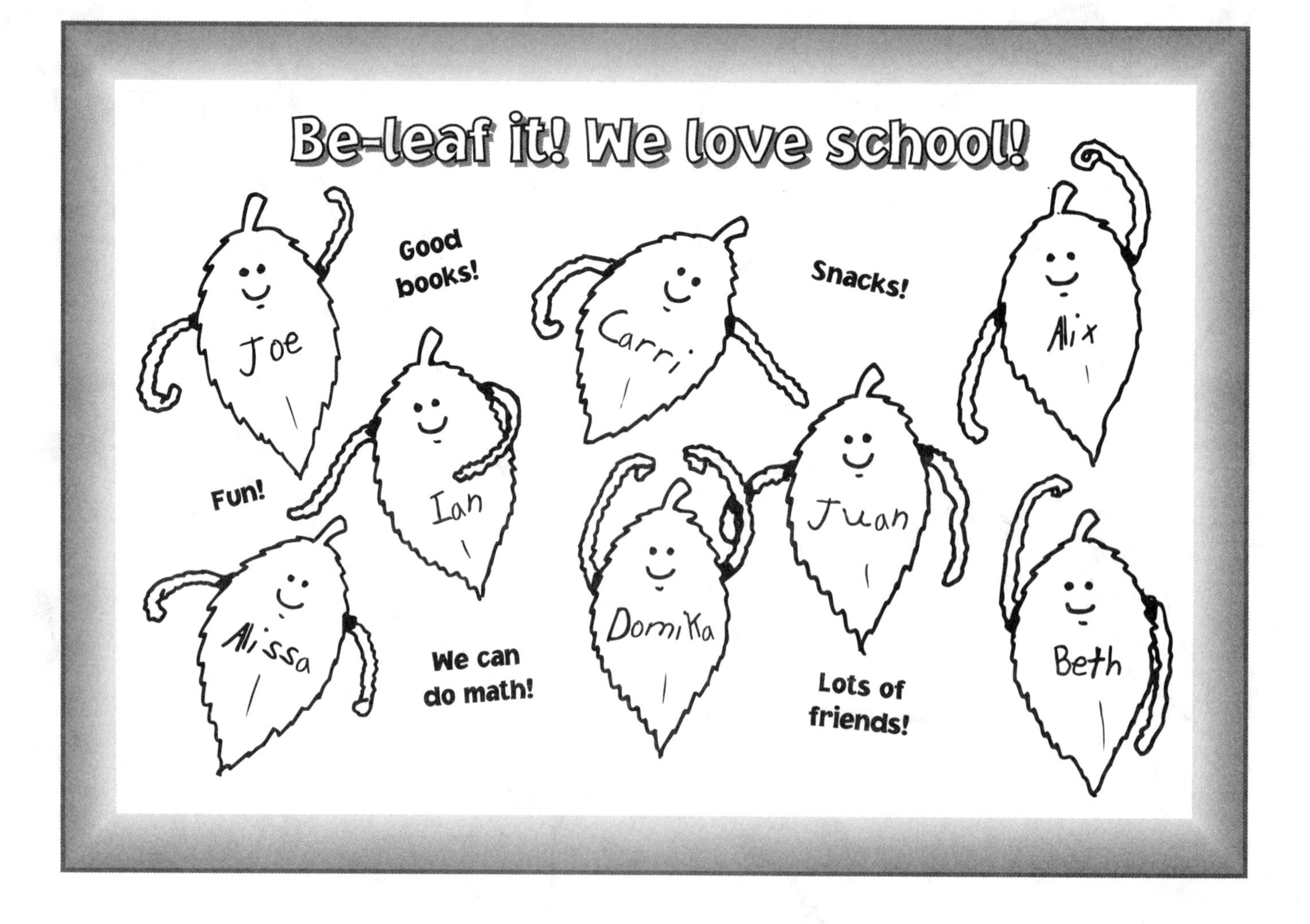

1. Cover the bulletin board with yellow paper. Reproduce the leaf pattern on page 7, one for each student. Use colored construction paper. Enlarge pattern as necessary to fit the board. Cut out the patterns and have children write their names on the leaves.

2. Then add pipe cleaner "arms" as illustrated. Attach to the board.

3. As a class, brainstorm reasons the children like school and write them on the board, using colored markers.

4. Add the title "Be-leaf it! We love school!" at the top of the board.

Bulletin Board Patterns

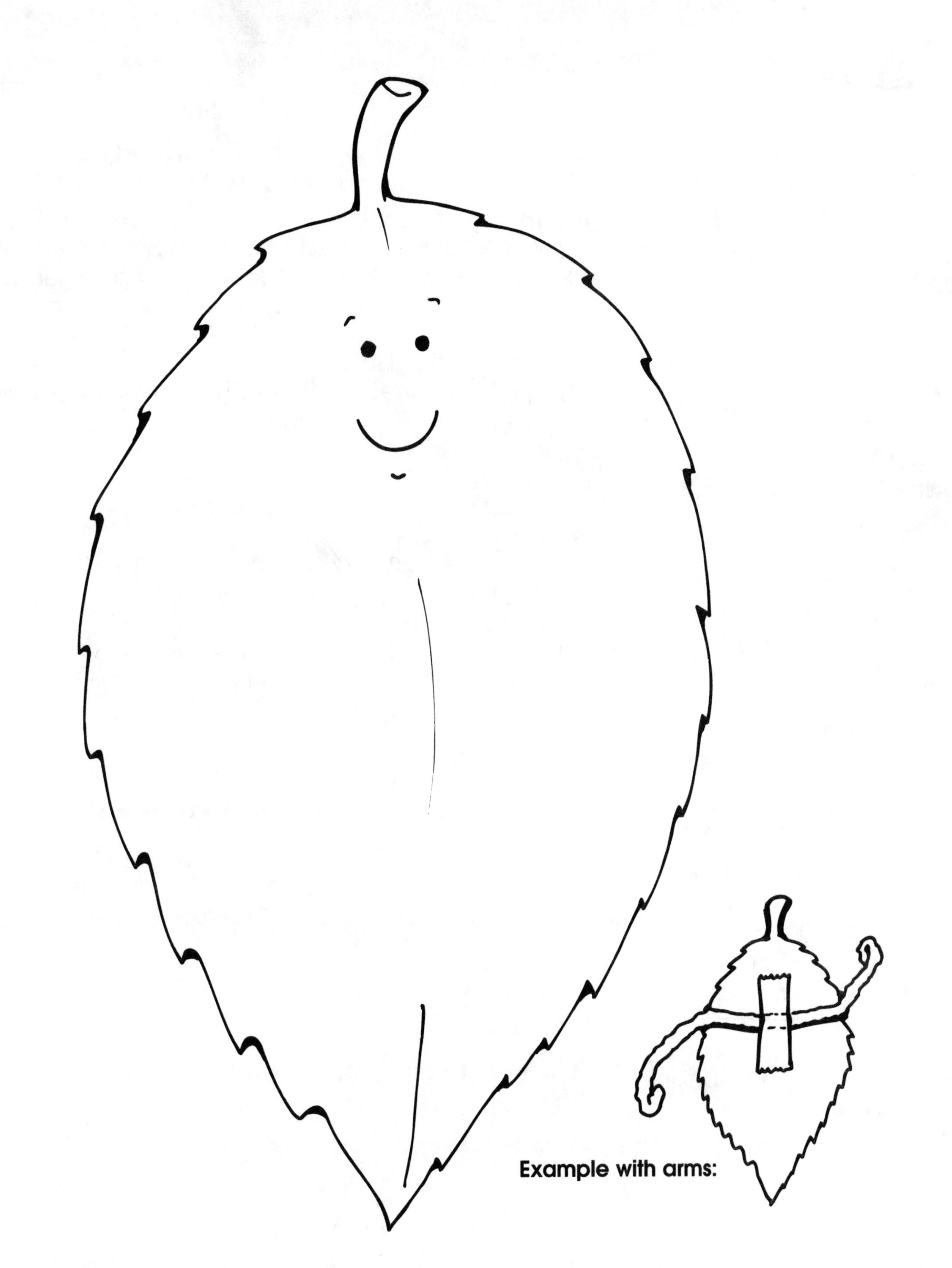

Poppleton in Fall

by Cynthia Rylant, Blue Sky Press, 1999

This early-reading adventure features the everyday antics of Poppleton the Pig. Three different stories make this a terrific addition to your library.

How Do You Know It's Fall? (Rookie Read-About Science)

by Allan Fowler, Children's Press, 1994

This is a great way to teach young children about the signs of fall. Simple language details geese flying south, squirrels hiding acorns and people playing football.

Picking Apples and Pumpkins

by Amy Hutchings, Cartwheel Books, 1994

This simple book describes a family outing to pick apples and pumpkins. The book shows fall activities like carving jack-o'-lanterns and baking apple pies. A great book for the classroom!

Too Many Pumpkins

by Linda White, Holiday House, 1997

This is a story about a woman who HATES pumpkins! Then one day a pumpkin falls off of a truck and squashes in her yard, sending seeds flying everywhere. Soon she has a lot of pumpkins. At first, she's horrified but then she discovers a way to make the best of the situation and discovers pumpkins are good after all.

Other Great Books:

Kids' Pumpkin Projects: Planting & Harvest Fun

by Deanna F. Cook, Williamson Publishing, 1998

Fall Harvest: Preparing for Winter

by Gail Saunders-Smith, Capstone Press, 1998

Hayride Fun

Reproduce the hay wagon and wheel patterns on pages 10 and 11. Color and cut out. Attach the wheels with brads and add a 6" piece of twine to the front of the wagon. Glue small pieces of raffia to create "hay" in the wagon.

Fingerpaint Indian Corn

Reproduce the corn pattern on page 10 and cut out. Using washable stamp pads, markers or poster paints in bright fall colors, have children use their fingertips to paint the Indian corn kernels. Then paint the husks or glue on dried corn husks. For a great classroom decoration, attach the ears of corn to real corn stalks and display.

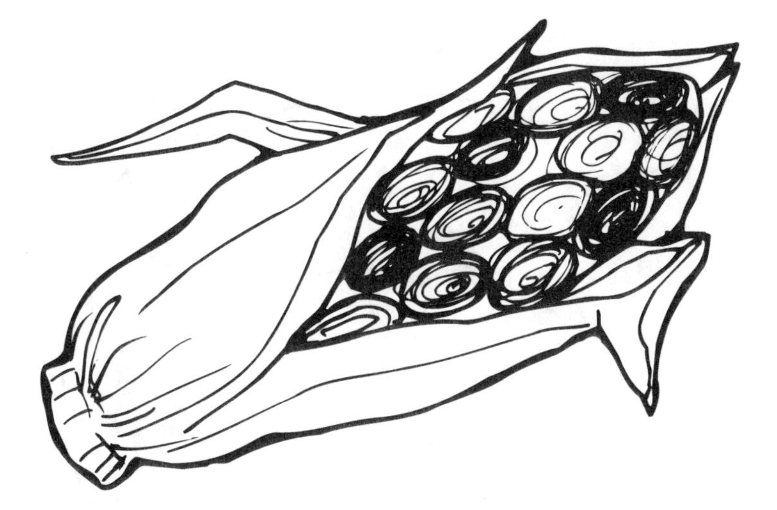

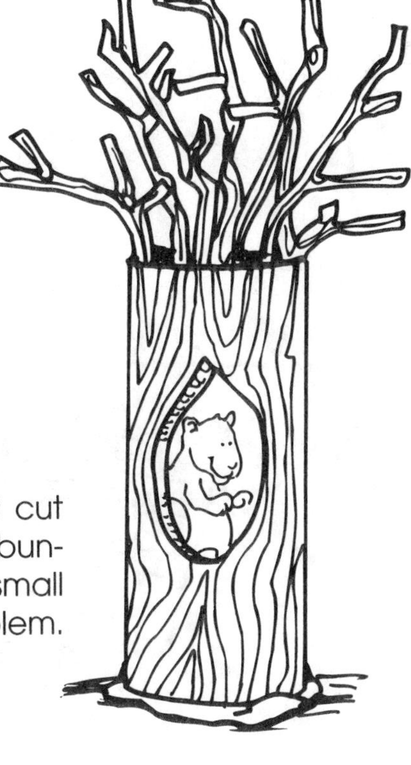

"Tree"mendous Fall

Reproduce the tree pattern on page 11. Color and cut out. Attach to an empty cardboard roll. Place a small bundle of bare twigs inside the roll, as illustrated. Use a small piece of clay to secure to the table if tipping is a problem.

Craft Patterns

Fingerpaint Indian Corn

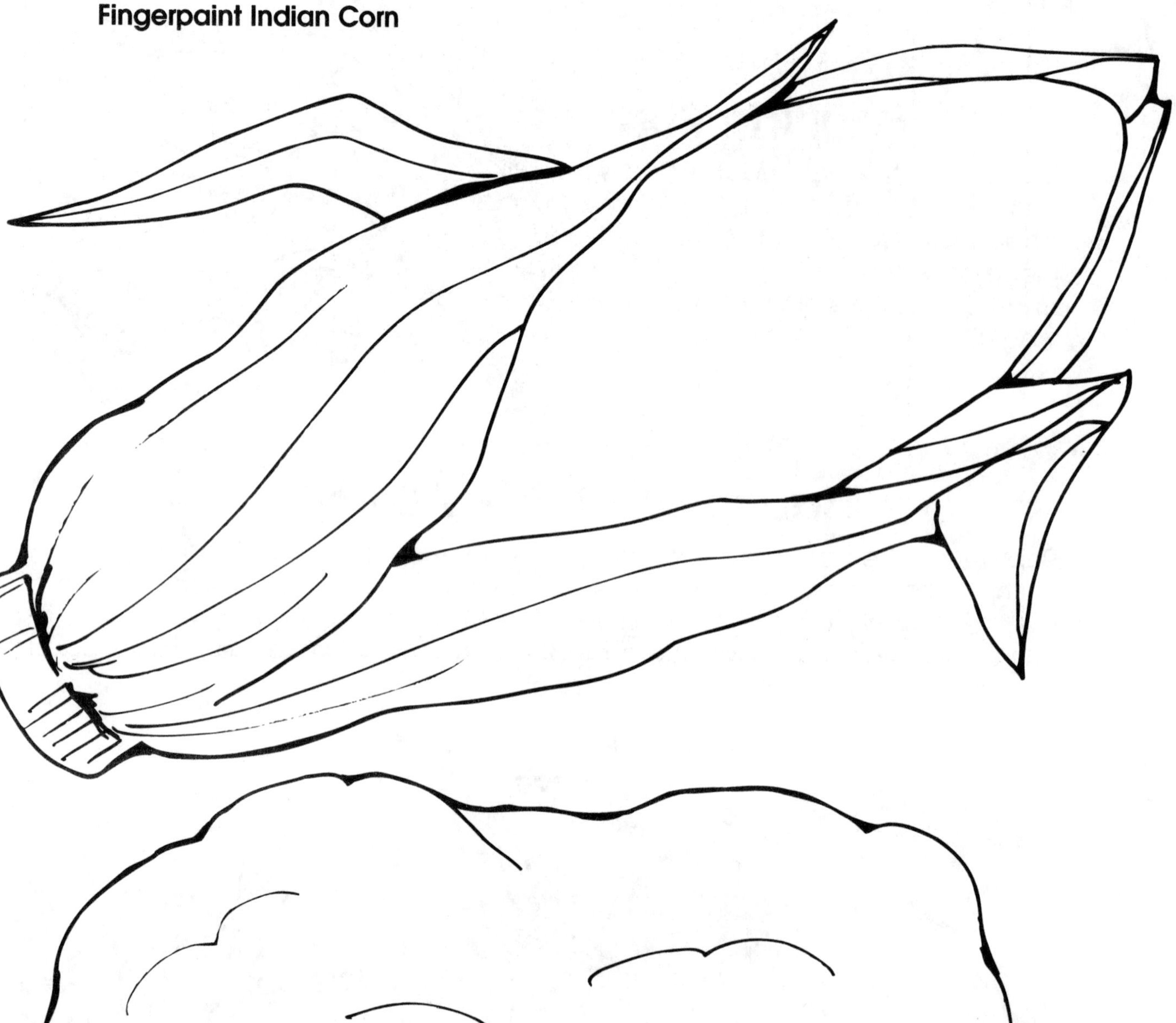

Hayride Fun

Craft Patterns

glue

"Tree"mendous Fall

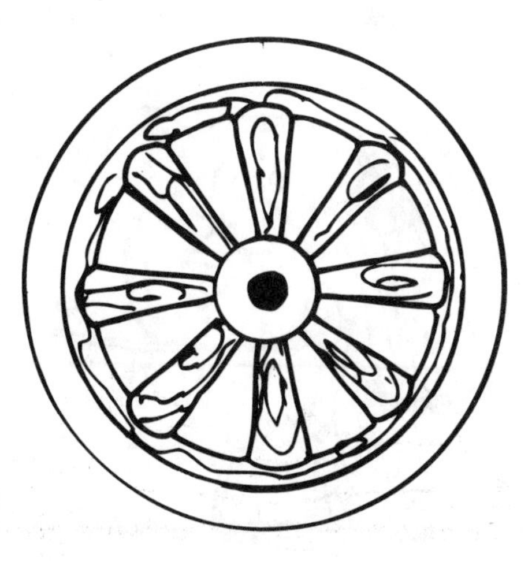

Hayride Fun

Fall
ACTION RHYME

Fall Fingerplay

5 golden leaves hanging from a tree,
(Put up 5 fingers, hand over head, swaying)
2 fell down and then there were 3.
(Put two fingers down and only sway three)

Now we pick corn, 1, 2, 3 and 4,
(Count with fingers)
How colorful it is! Let's pick more!
(Look around and pretend to pick more)

6 big pumpkins grow ripe at harvesttime,
(Put up 6 fingers and sit down)
I see 3 more, and now there are 9!
(Jump up showing 9 fingers)

We pick juicy apples, 6, 7, 8, 9,10,
(Lick your lips)
We eat them for a snack so we'll have to pick again!
(Pretend to eat an apple)

The leaves fell off the tree. Now I see only 1.
(Put up one finger)
Counting through the harvest is really fun!
(Count to 10)

Cornucopia Lunch

Roll the top edge of a small brown lunch bag back and crumple the bottom into a point to form a paper cornucopia. Insert a snack-sized paper plate into the rolled edge and use this to serve a pint-sized harvest snack!

Autumn Leaves

Cut assorted slices of cheeses and lunch meats into leaf shapes, using cookie cutters. Serve the leaves on fall-colored paper plates with leaf-shaped snack crackers and pretzel "twigs."

Hot and Cold Lunch

Serve a snack of opposites. Using a hollowed-out pumpkin or large squash as a bowl, serve vegetable soup to the children. From another pumpkin or squash bowl, serve a cold vegetable salad. Discuss the differences. You could also expand the exploration of tastes by serving crunchy crackers and soft, chewy bread, or sweet cookies with tart lemon spread.

⚠ Make sure you are aware of any food allergies or restrictions students may have. Be sure children wash their hands before they eat.

Fall is harvesttime. Draw 5 apples on the tree.

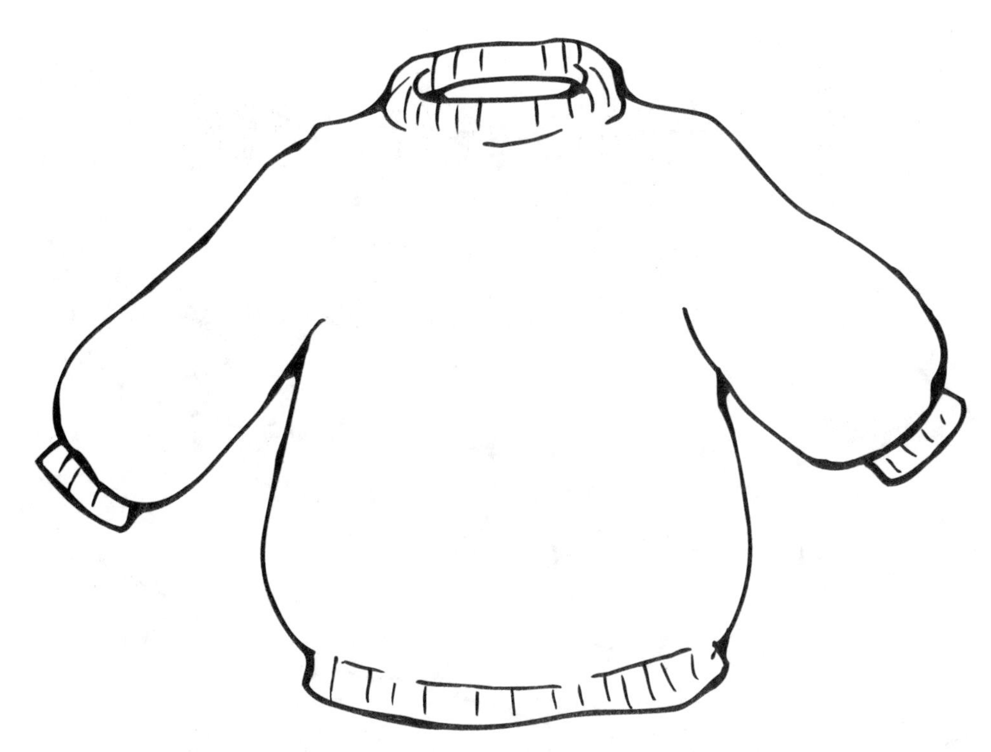

Fall is chilly. Decorate the sweater with pretty fall colors.

2

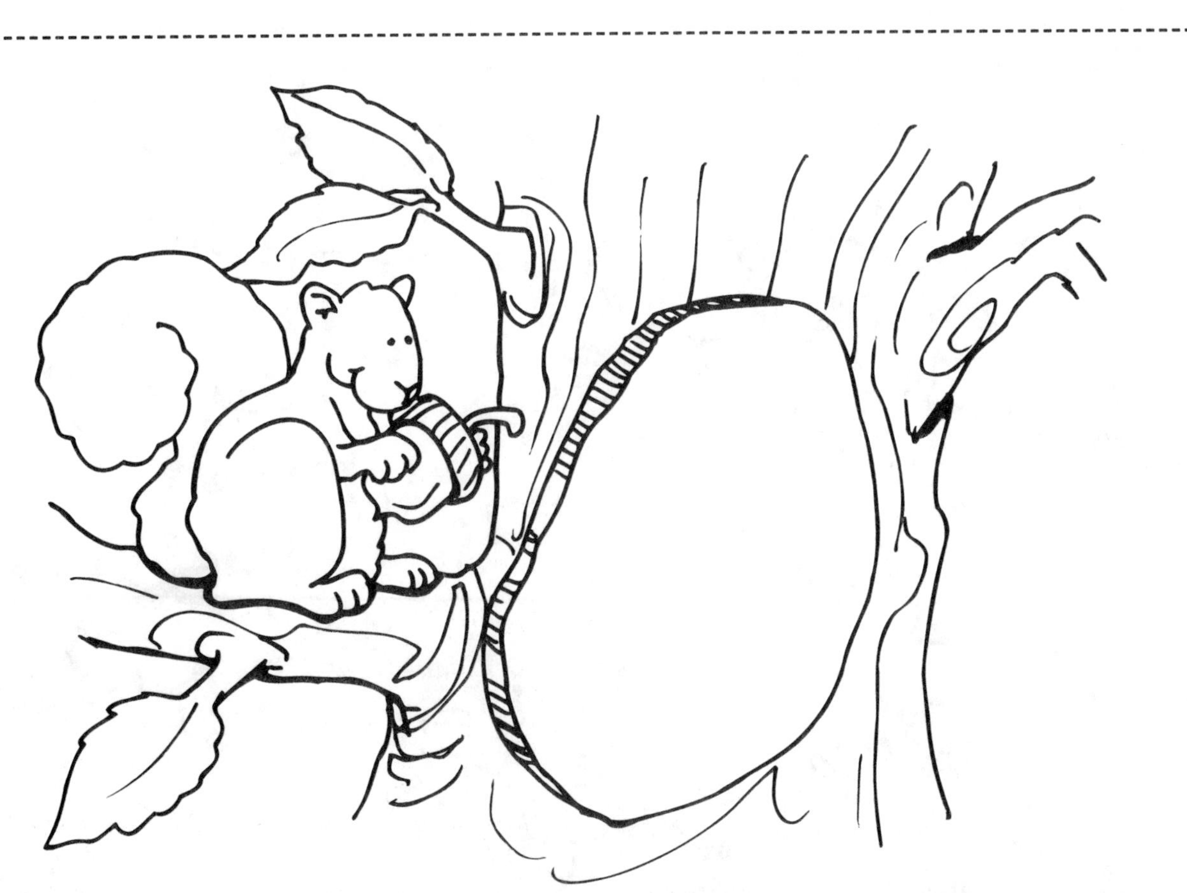

Squirrels gather nuts for winter. Can you draw 3 acorns in the hole?

3

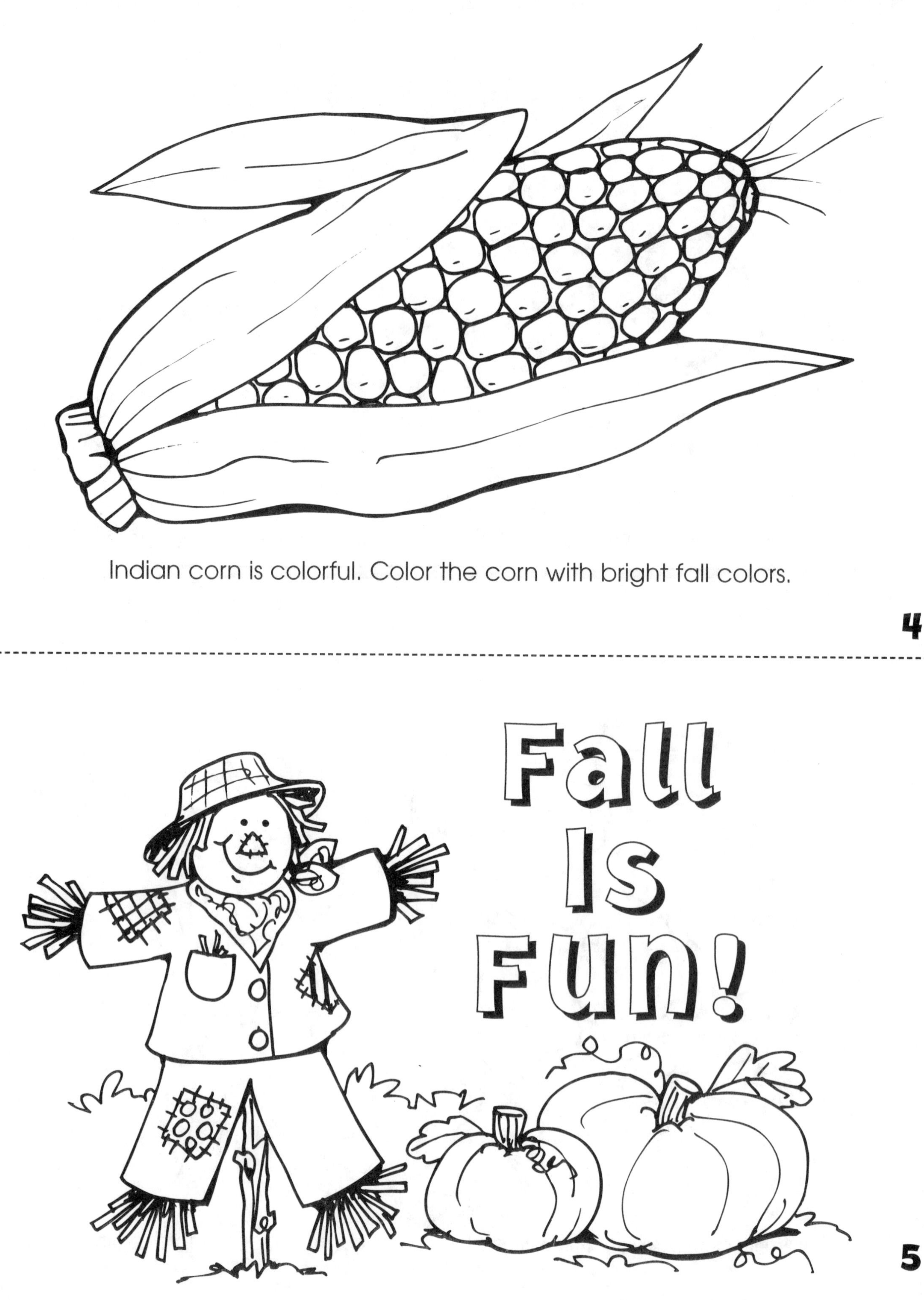

Indian corn is colorful. Color the corn with bright fall colors.

4

5

Name

Scarecrow Fun

Decorate and color the scarecrow. Be sure to give him a face!

Name

Colorful Fun

Color the pictures the correct color.

Name

Count and Color

Color the first rake blue.
Color the sixth rake green.

Color the third rake red.
Color the second rake orange.

Color 2 pumpkins green.
Color 1 pumpkin orange.

Color 3 pumpkins yellow.

Color the third leaf orange.
Color the second leaf red.

Color the sixth leaf green.
Color the fourth leaf yellow.

Color one acorn red.
Color two acorns pink.

Color two acorns purple.
Color one acorn blue.

Name

Number Skills

Count the objects in each set.
Circle the number that shows how many are in each set.

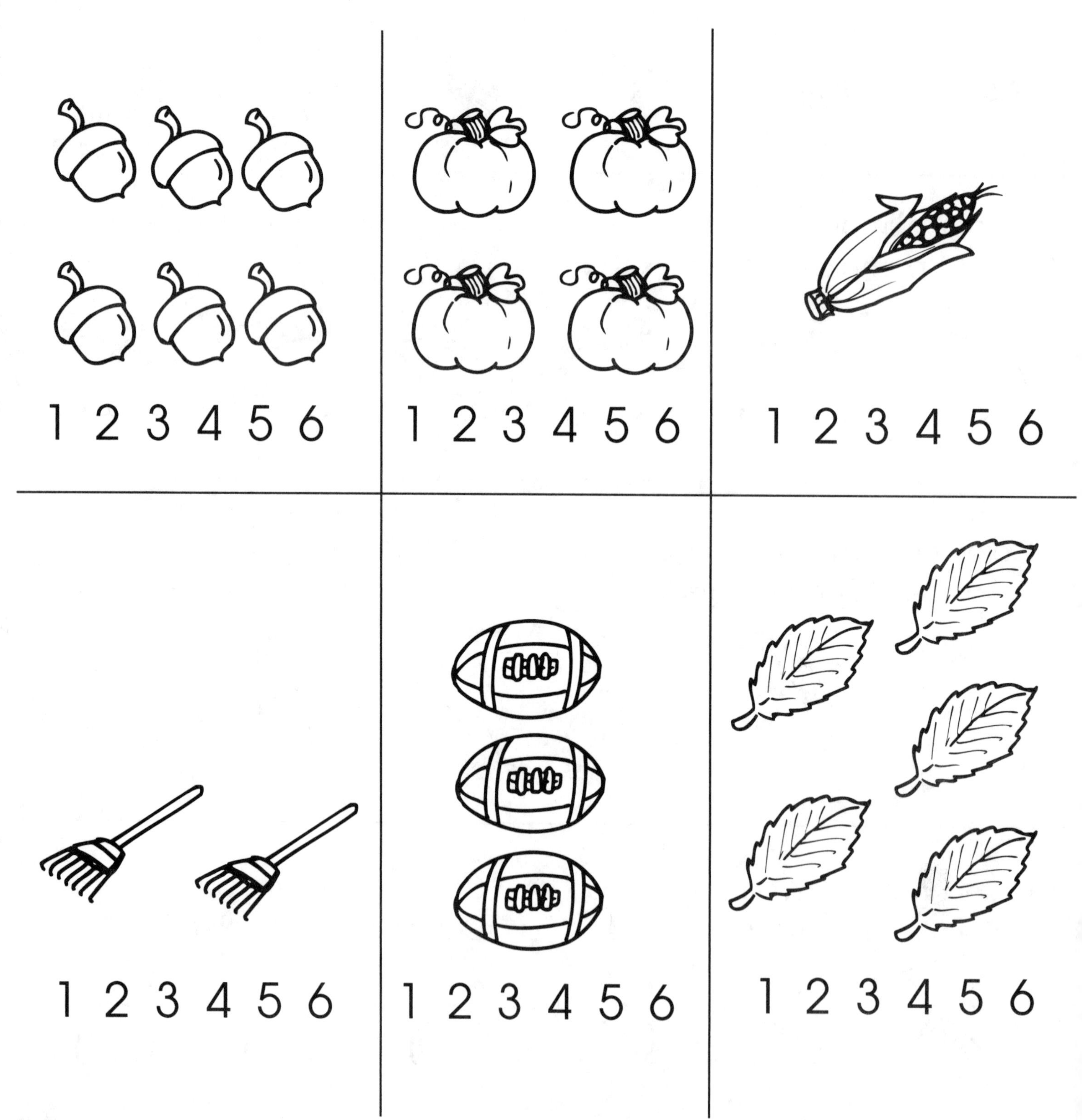

Name

Fall Dot-to-Dot

Follow the numbers to complete this fall picture.

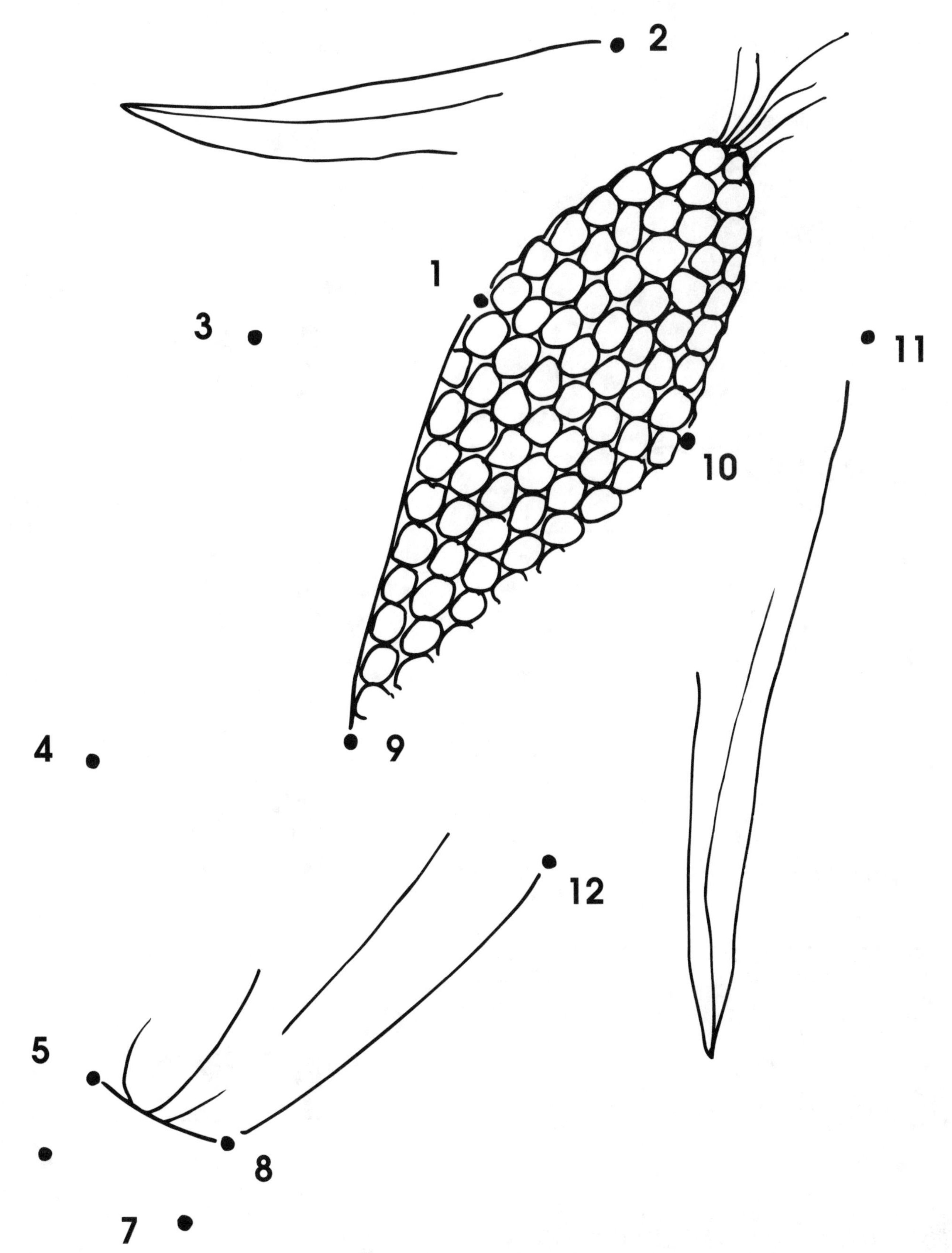

Name

Matching Sounds

Look at the pictures. Think of the letter that makes the first sound of each one.
Draw a line from the picture to the correct letter.

Name

Fall Maze

Can you help the bird find the ear of corn?

Name ____________________________________

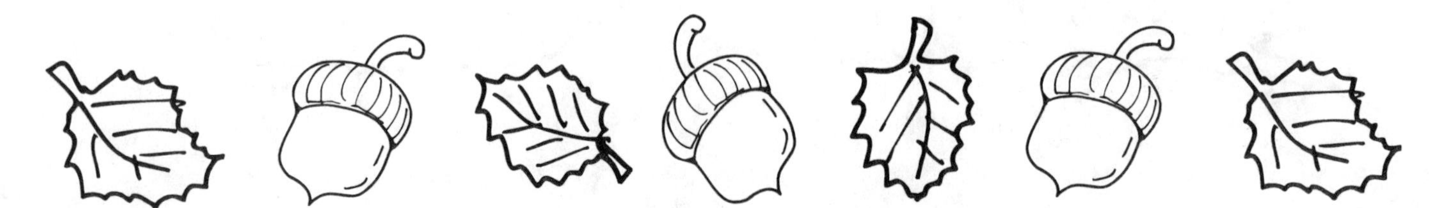

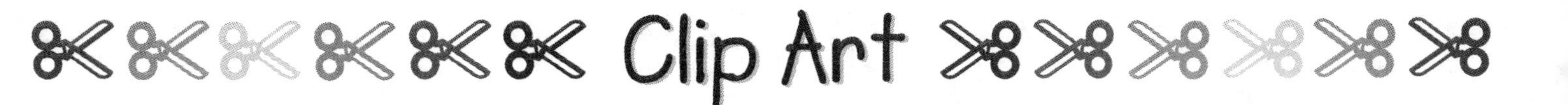

Clip Art

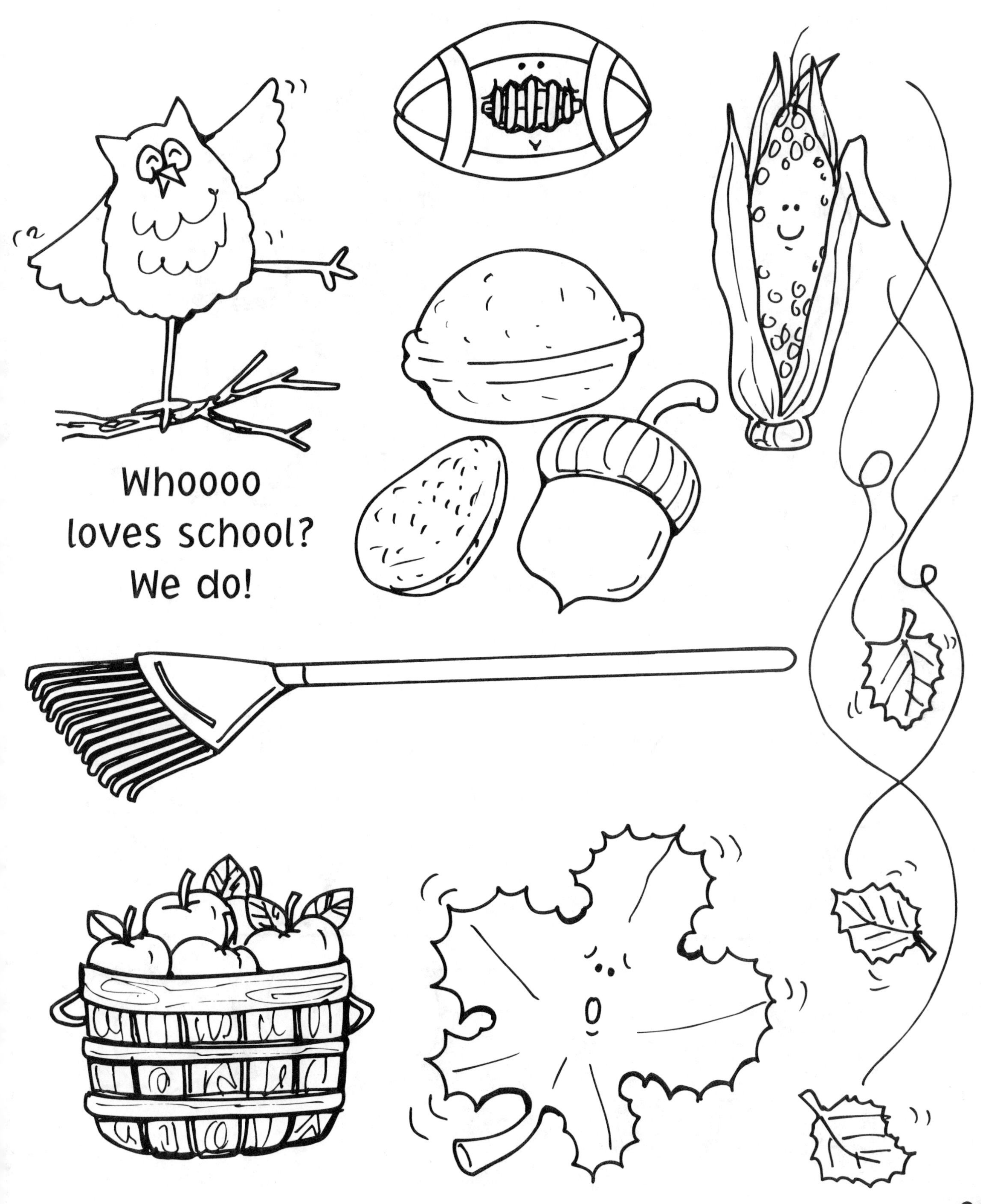

Clip Art

Book Cover

Name ______________________________

Fall Poster to Color

Activities

Pumpkin Placement

Copy the large pumpkin pattern on page 31 and make two copies of the smaller pumpkin pattern on page 31 on orange paper. Cut one set for each for child. Use the pumpkins to practice following instructions. For example, say "Put the small pumpkin above the big pumpkin" or "Hide the little pumpkin behind the big pumpkin."

My Pumpkin's Name Is . . .

After the children complete the "Design a Jack-o'-Lantern" project on page 45, use the finished project to practice creative thinking and letter recognition skills. Have children take turns naming their pumpkin and finding one thing the pumpkin likes based on the first letter of its name. For example: My pumpkin's name is **A**dam and he likes **a**lligators!" or "My pumpkin's name is **J**ackie and she likes **j**uice!" This can be easily expanded depending on the skill level, to include where the pumpkin lives, its favorite food, etc.

Sweep Away the Spiders

Reproduce the broom and 5-10 spiders from patterns provided on page 31. Cut out one set for each child. Give simple math problems based on "sweeping" the spiders under the broom. For example: "You have six spiders and you sweep up two. How many spiders are still running around?" or "Four spiders are hiding under your broom. One spider escapes. How many spiders are still hiding?"

Match the Half

Draw a jack-o'-lantern on a sheet of paper or use the pattern provided on page 31. Fold down the center of the pumpkin. Reproduce only the half drawing on a full sheet of paper, one copy for each child. Let each child complete the jack-o'-lantern, trying to match the pattern. Then children should color their finished drawings.

"Batty" About Numbers!

Make 10-20 copies of the bat pattern on page 31. Write the numbers 1-10 or 1-20 in the center of the bats and mix them up. Let each child pick one bat and clip it, with a clothespin, to a yarn line. Encourage the children to hang the bats in numerical order. Continue until all the bats are "flying."

Halloween Sort and Count

Make multiple copies of the clip art on pages 51 and 52 and cut the pictures apart. Mix the sets together and give each child a small pile of Halloween shapes to sort and count. Children can switch piles and repeat the process. Older children can graph their results.

Activities Patterns

Bulletin Board

1. Cover the bulletin board with black paper. Reproduce the moon and leaf patterns on page 33 enlarging as necessary to fit your board. Color and cut out. Also, reproduce the jack-o'-lantern pattern on page 33, one for each child.

2. Have students decorate, color and cut out the jack-o'-lanterns. Then children should write their names on the back. With a paper punch, punch a hole in each pumpkin stem. Loop a small piece of green yarn through the hole and tie it into a bow.

3. Add green yarn vines and the leaves, as shown, to create your class pumpkin patch. Attach the moon and add the title, "Whooooooooo's in the Pumpkin Patch?"

4. Attach the pumpkins to the board, by the yarn bows, so children and guests can try to guess who made each pumpkin, and then turn it over to check their guess.

Bulletin Board Patterns

Books

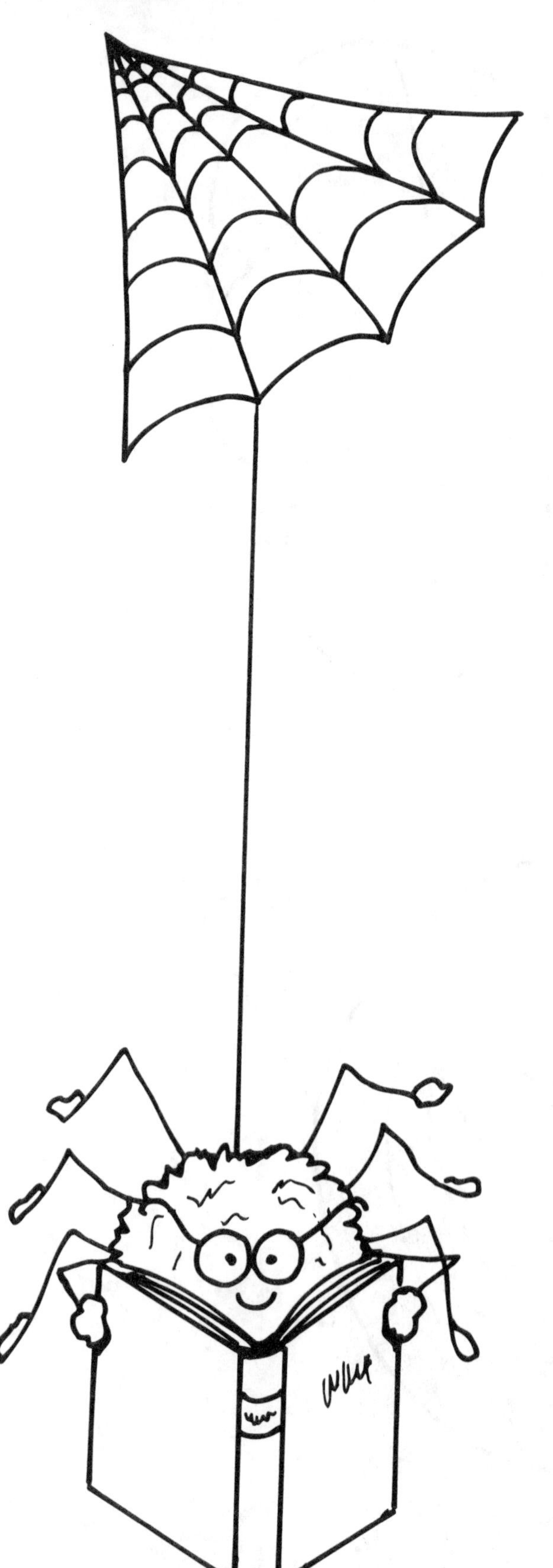

Jeb Scarecrow's Pumpkin Patch

by Jana Dillon, Houghton Mifflin, 1992

Jeb Scarecrow comes up with an ingenious plan to keep the pesky crows from having their October celebration in his pumpkin patch. A delightful book for both children and grown-ups.

The Biggest Pumpkin Ever

by Steven Kroll, Cartwheel Books, 1993

This story is about two mice who fall in love with the same pumpkin. They each take care of the pumpkin, and don't know the other one is doing the same. This book is a great way to show how pumpkins grow.

Angelina's Halloween

by Katharine Holabird, Pleasant Co. Publications, 2000

A perfect book for preschoolers with just the right mix of spookiness and other Halloween fun. The story includes trick-or-treating, a Halloween parade, and other Halloween traditions. Angelina and her friend must deal with Angelina's little sister tagging along and learn an important lesson at the end of the story.

Scary, Scary Halloween

by Eve Bunting, illus. by Jan Brett, Clarion Publishing, 1986

Fun-filled rhymes and bright, colorful illustrations make this a wonderful book for young children.

Other Good Books:

Tiny Teeny Halloweeny Treasury
by Mary Engelbreit, Andrews McMeel Publishing, 2001
Halloween School Parties: What Do I Do?
by Wihelminia Ripple, Oakbrook Publishing House, 1996
101 Spooktacular Party Ideas
by Linda Sadler, Creative Kids Products, 2000

Starry Night

Use a 6" paper plate as a template to cut an arc out of a 9" paper plate to create a moon for each child. Reproduce three stars for each moon, using the patterns provided on page 36. Have children color the moon and stars yellow. Add gold glitter if desired. Punch holes and attach the stars to the moon as illustrated.

Batty Windsock

Glue six 18" strips of black crepe paper to the bottom edge of a 9" paper plate. Fold in half and staple edges shut. Color the paper plate black. Cut small triangles out of the stapled edges to make a bat's wings as shown. Glue two of the scrap triangles to the folded edge to create ears. Add two white eyes and draw a mouth. Use a string for hanging.

Busy, Busy Broom

Reproduce the broom pattern on page 36. Color and cut out. Fold strands of tan raffia in half and glue to broom pattern as shown, adding as many as needed to cover pattern. Trim raffia ends so they are even with the bottom of the pattern. Add a line of white glue and sprinkle with glitter to "wire" the broom bristles together.

Craft Patterns

Halloween
ACTION RHYME

Halloween Puppet Play

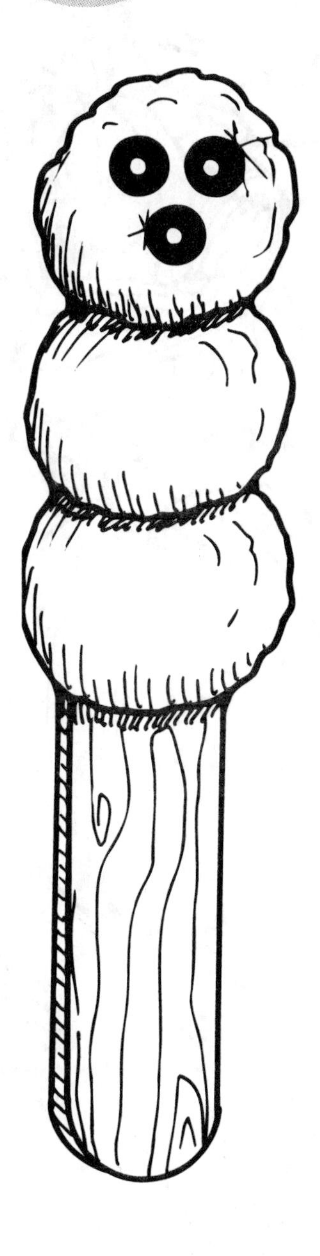

Little ghost, little ghost, come out to play.
(Children use one hand to hide puppet behind their backs.)

Where are you hiding this Halloween day?
(Children put their free hand over their eyes and look from side to side.)

Little ghost, little ghost, peek at me.
(Children peek through their fingers.)

It's trick-or-treat time, just look and see!
(Children open their eyes wide.)

Little ghost, little ghost, it's almost night,
(Children close their eyes.)

Time to jump out and give me a fright!
(Children pretend to look scared.)

Little ghost, little ghost, where are you?
(Repeat hand over the eyes looking from side to side.)

Here I am . . . ready . . . set . . . BOO!
(Children say "Here I am . . . ready . . .set . . ." in a low spooky voice and then pull out puppets from behind their backs as they yell "Boo!")

To make ghost puppets: Glue three big cotton balls in a row on a large craft stick. Then glue three black sequins to the top cotton ball to make the eyes and mouth.

A Kitten's Halloween

A little, black kitten bravely set out
To discover what Halloween was all about.

He followed some children in funny clothes,
And thought, "I'll find out where everyone goes."

They knocked on a door and said, "Trick or Treat!"
And had their bags filled with candy to eat.

Then suddenly, the black kitten spied
A big, smiling pumpkin with a candle inside.

It looked very cheerful, but it couldn't talk,
So the kitten left and continued his walk.

Just then a loud scream rang through the night,
And the kitten's hair stood up in fright.

The children weren't scared, not even one.
But the kitten decided his exploring was done.

He hurried for home as fast as could be,
And said, "Halloween is for kids, and not for me!"

I'd rather be home with my sister and brother,
All cozy and safe, right next to my mother."

Snacks

Creepy, Crunchy Snack Mix

In small zipper bag, mix candy corn, popcorn, cereal and gummy worms together. Decorate the bag with Halloween stickers and personalized name tags.

"Buggy" Stew

Mix several drops of green or blue food coloring into a bowl of applesauce. Add raisin "bugs" and small pieces of chopped bananas or other soft fruit. Top with a gummy spider or two.

Pumpkin Yogurt Cups

Cut the top off a small orange and scoop out the inside. Draw a jack-o'-lantern face, with a black, permanent marker on one side of the orange. Mix vanilla yogurt and a little bit of the orange pulp together in a bowl and re-fill the hollowed out orange. Replace the cut-off top and top with a candy spearmint leaf.

⚠ Make sure you are aware of any food allergies or restrictions children may have. Be sure children wash their hands, and fruits and vegetables before they eat.

Draw 3 pumpkins in the pumpkin patch.

1

Can you see the bat fly? Then color it black.

Decorate this
trick-or-treat bag.

How many spider legs can you count?
Add 5 legs so it has 8!

4

5

Name

Colorful Fun

Color each picture the correct color.

Name

Count and Color

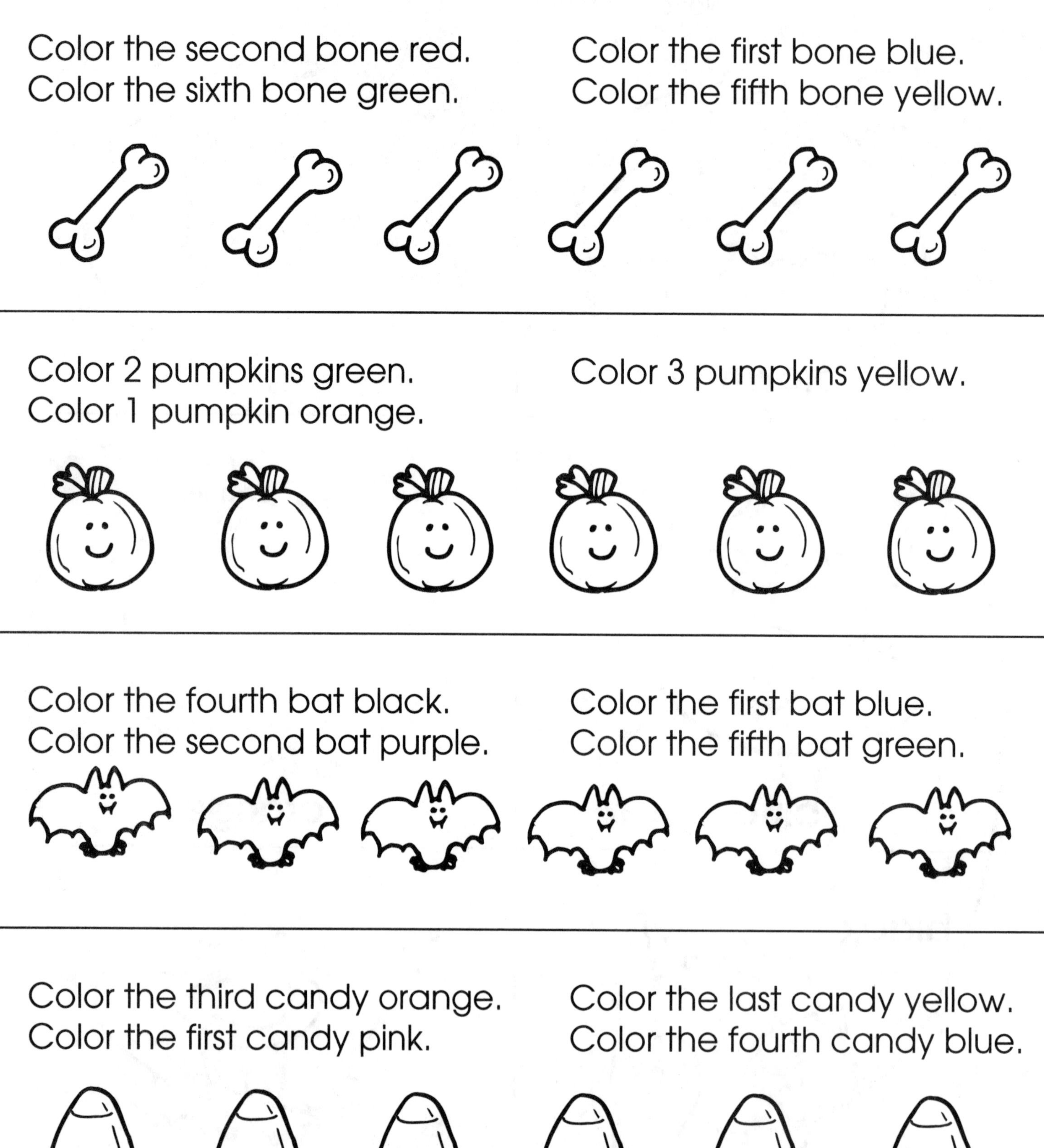

Name

Design a Jack-o'-Lantern

Name

Number Skills

Count the objects in each set.
Circle the number that shows how many are in each set.

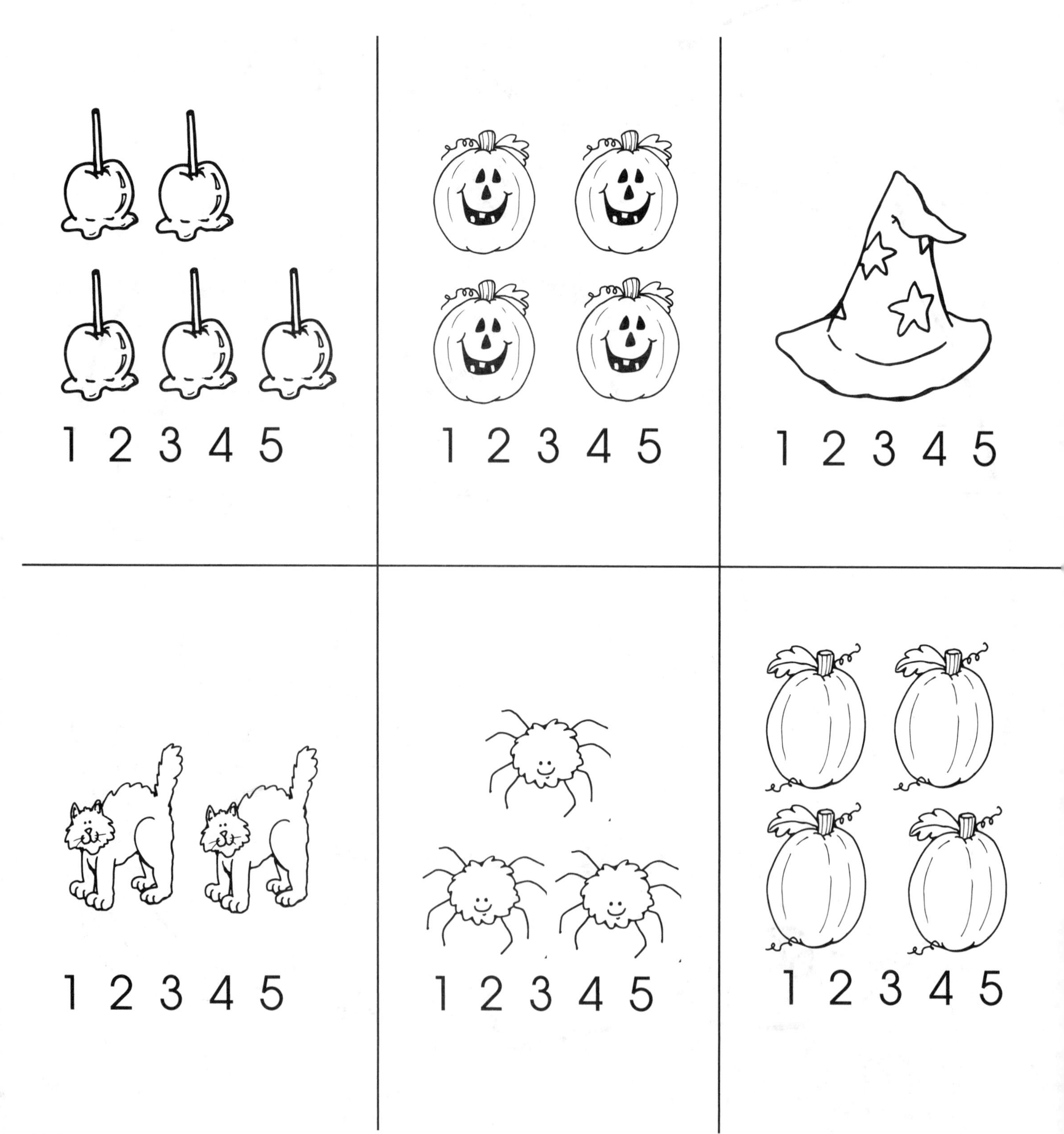

Name

Dot-to-Dot

Follow the numbers to see what's shining on Halloween night.

Name

Matching Sounds

Look at the pictures. Think of the letter that makes the first sound of each. Draw a line from the picture to the correct letter.

Ss

Cc

Bb

Mm

Pp

Name

Halloween Maze

Can you help the mouse get to his pumpkin house?

Name ______________________________

Clip Art

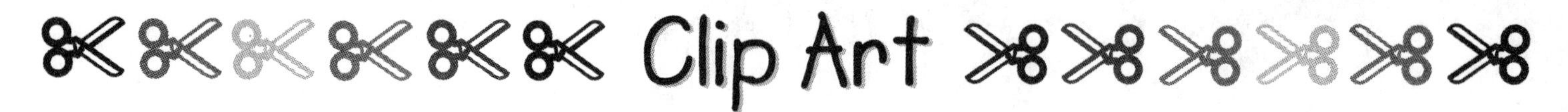
Clip Art

HAVE A
SPOOKY
HALLOWEEN!

Book Cover

Name ______________________________

Halloween Poster to Color

Graph the Winter Snowfall

Give each child a copy of the "Snow Watch Activity Sheet" on page 59. After a snowfall, have children print the date of the snowfall at the bottom of the graph. Then check a snow gauge, local newspaper or weather channel to see how much snow has fallen. Show children how to color the correct number of inches of snow on their graph with crayons.

If you live in an area without snow, pick a city or state that does get a lot of snow and gather your data from the Internet at www.weather.com.

Where Do Animals Go in the Winter?

Draw a picture of the forest in the winter on a sheet of construction paper. Cut out pictures of different animals from magazines or catalogs. Use these pictures to show where the animals spend their winter. For example, place a bear inside a cave. Here are a few tips about winter animals:

- Squirrels, chipmunks, mice, raccoons, and groundhogs find hollow trees or logs to sleep in during cold winter months.
- Insects hibernate as larvae, grubs, eggs, or cocoons that are attached to bark, twigs, or under rocks. These insects are frozen solid during this time.
- Turtles and frogs bury themselves in mud.
- Snakes and lizards hibernate in holes or rocky dens.
- Hibernating birds include chimney swifts, quail and grouse. Other birds migrate south.
- Some animals stay active in winter, such as rabbits, deer, wolves, fox, owls and squirrels.
- Bees and ants seal the entrance to their hives and nests.

Make a Snow Gauge

You Will Need
wide-mouth jar
length of masking tape
pen or marker
ruler
"Snow Watch Activity Sheet" on page 59

Cut a length of masking tape that extends from the bottom of the jar to the top. Using a ruler, mark the masking tape with lines at quarter-inch increments. Attach the masking tape to the side of the jar. Place the jar outside away from buildings or trees. After a snowfall, record the amount of snow in the jar on your "Snow Watch Activity Sheet."

Outdoor Fun

Find pictures of outdoor winter activities, such as sledding, tobogganing, ice skating, skiing, playing hockey or walking in the snow. Discuss the pictures with the children.

1. What is happening in each picture?
2. What clothing is worn for each activity? What equipment is used?
3. How many people are participating in each activity?
4. Which activities require skill and practice?
5. Who has participated in any of these winter activities?

Stop and Tell

Begin telling a story about winter and stop in the middle. Then let the children take turns telling the rest of the story. For example, "One day it was snowing. The children put on their winter clothes and went out to play. All of a sudden, ..."

Winter Walk

Take children on a winter walk. Choose a nice day, but be sure to dress warmly. You can walk to a local park or just go out to the playground. Then ask children questions about winter.

What is different about the trees? How did they look in spring? In fall? What about the grass—how is it different? What color is it? Are there puddles in the streets or parking lot? Is there ice? Can you lift up rocks or are they frozen to the ground? If you can lift them, what is under them? What do you think will be under them in summer?

Have students describe the sky. *What color is it? What do the clouds look like?*

Look for animals. If there aren't a lot of animals, have students tell what they know about the winter habits of animals.

Talk about the temperature. *How does the air feel on your face? Your hands? Your tongue? How did it feel in summer? What are some things we do in winter to stay warm? How did you stay cool in summer?*

If there's snow on the ground, put a few flakes on a piece of black paper. Explain that each snowflake is unique. After your walk, have students cut out snowflakes from folded paper. See if they can make any that are exactly alike.

Talk to students about winter weather and how we must be careful when traveling during snowstorms. Explain the importance of covering exposed skin when it is very cold. Ask if any students know stories of people who had trouble when traveling during winter or who have had frostbite. Discuss why it is more difficult for cars to stop on ice.

Ask students what they like to do outside during the winter.

Indoor Fun

Once you've returned from your Winter Walk, ask children what they can do inside in the winter.

Here are some suggestions:

- Start a jigsaw puzzle on a table in the back of the room for children to work on during free time or indoor recess.

- Mechanical puzzles that require thinking skills like moving one metal oval through another offer a good indoor diversion on cold, snowy days.

- Create a cozy reading corner using pillows and carpet squares or create a "cave" inside a huge cardboard box. Keep a stack of great books close by.

- Play card games during free time. Include old favorites like Go Fish, Old Maid and Uno™.

- Start a winter garden. Have each child decorate a Styrofoam™ cup. Fill the cups with potting soil and have children plant radish seeds in them. Place the cups on a tabletop near windows, but not in sills right next to glass. Water the plants with a spray bottle so as not to damage the tiny plants. Help children nurture their winter garden.

- Teach children to play dominoes or dice games such as Bunco or Yahtzee. These games are not only fun, but they will also help reinforce early math skills.

- Bring some garden and seed catalogs to class for children to see. Have them choose pictures of vegetables, fruits, and flowers. Then they can cut out and paste the pictures on construction paper to create a garden that they would like to plant.

- Play a game of "Name That Picture." Write winter words (*snow, snowman, sled, coat, sweater, icicle, skiing, hat, hockey, mittens, snowsuit, soup, hot chocolate*) on index cards (one word per card).

  Choose two teams. Have a child from each team choose an index card. Then the two children should go to the board and try to draw their words. Their teams should try to guess what word they are drawing. The first team to guess gets a point. Use a timer if necessary.

  You can also use this game for words you are studying in social studies or science units. Try to use nouns because verbs and adjectives are harder for children to draw.

Snow Watch Activity Sheet

_______ _______ _______ _______ _______ _______

Date of Snowfall

Bulletin Board

1. Cover a bulletin board with blue paper. Then use white paper to add snow at the bottom. Reproduce the snowman pattern on page 61, enlarging as necessary to fit your board. Make 3-5 snowmen. Color, cut out and add to the board.

2. Encourage children to create their own snowflake for the board. They should put their name on the snowflake.

3. Add the snowflakes to the board and put the title *Winter Wonderland* across the top.

Bulletin Board Pattern

Books

The Three Snow Bears

by Jan Brett, Penguin Young Readers Group, 2007

A wintry version of "Goldilocks and the Three Bears," three polar bears go for a walk and save Aloo-ki's dogs while the little girl finds their home. Children will enjoy this beautiful picture book.

The Biggest Snowman Ever

by Steven Kroll, Scholastic, 2005

Two little mice learn the value of teamwork as they work together to build the biggest snowman ever.

Stranger in the Woods

by Carl R. Sams and Jean Stoick, Carl Sams Photography, 2000

This photographic book shows how animals and birds react to a snowman who suddenly appears in the woods after a winter storm. Children will love the photographs and the animals' reactions.

The Mitten

by Alvin R. Tresselt, HarperCollins Publishers, 1989

This beautifully illustrated book tells the story of a little boy who drops his mitten in the woods on the coldest day of the year. Animals use the mitten for warmth and it stretches and stretches to hold them all.

Other Good Books:

Danny's First Snow
by Leonid Gore, Simon & Schuster, 2007

Owl Moon
by Jane Yolen, Penguin Young Readers Group, 1987

The Snowy Day
by Ezra Jack Keats, Penguin Group, 1996

Painting with Pine Boughs

Use small pine boughs as paintbrushes. Place a small bough beside containers of different colored tempera paints. Dip the end of a pine bough in the paint. Stroke it across the page or press down as a stamp. Or, dip the side of a pinecone in paint and brush the cone across the page to create interesting designs. Ask children to think of other natural materials that can be used as paintbrushes.

Ice Painting with Gelatin

Get your class in a creative mood as they try a new way of painting. First, prepare ice paintbrushes. Fill an ice cube tray with water and cover the top with aluminum foil. Insert craft sticks in the cube sections through the foil. Freeze overnight. Give each child a sheet of white paper. Then, sprinkle a small amount of powdered gelatin on the paper. Use several flavors if you wish. Have children paint over the gelatin with an ice cube "paintbrush." What happens? How does it smell?

Animal in the Snow

Combine art and science with this project. Provide nature magazines for children to use to find animals they might see in winter. They should cut out the animal pictures and glue them on construction paper or poster board. Then have children paint the pictures with a solution of 1 cup Epsom salts and ½ cup water. When the picture dries, a frosty coating (ice crystals) will make the animals look like they're in the snow!

Snowflake Ornament

Glue wheel-shaped pasta together in a snowflake shape on top of waxed paper. Everyone's snowflake will be slightly different. When the glue dries, paint the snowflake with white tempera paint. For sparkle, add white or silver glitter while the paint is still wet. When thoroughly dry, slide string or yarn thorough one of the wheel holes and hang in the classroom!

Winter Puffy Paint

Mix equal amounts of shaving cream (non-menthol) and white glue to make a puffy paint. This will look nice on pictures that require snow and will give the picture a 3D effect. Have children apply the puffy paint with fingers or a craft stick. They can also add snowballs to a winter drawing to create a puffy snowman. The paint can be tinted with food coloring if necessary.

Model Igloo

Children can make igloos from sugar cubes. Have them glue sugar cubes to one another on a cardboard platform. They can also use glitter, crystal studs and sequins to decorate the igloo. If you want to preserve the igloos, brush shellac on them. Adult supervision and adequate ventilation is needed when using shellac.

Inside and Outside

Winter is a fun time I know.
We can sled and play in the snow.

In winter, everything's covered in white,
And there are fewer hours of daylight.

Birds fly south and bears go to sleep.
It snows on the sidewalk, and the piles are deep!

The weather in winter is very cold.
"Bundle up in warm clothes," is what I am told!

So I put on my boots and my coat and my hat,
And outside, I go to see where the fun is at.

Soon I come back for the mittens I forgot,
Then hurry back out because inside it's too hot!

Name ______________________

In Wintertime. . .

some birds go south.	the sun takes longer naps.
bears go to sleep.	the trees are bare.
squirrels eat the food they've stored.	water freezes.
	animals get thicker coats.

Be creative. Draw pictures of what these things might look like. Use another sheet of paper if you want.

Wintertime Fun Song

To the tune of "On Top of Old Smokey"
Let children make up their own actions to this song as they sing it.

Snow falls on rooftops,
Then melts in the sun,
And icicles drip down
On everyone.

The snow softly lands on
The branches of trees,
And when I walk under,
It falls down on me.

If I roll some snowballs
As big as I can,
And put them together,
I'll have a snowman.

I'll give him a hat and
A nose and two eyes.
When my mother sees him,
Won't she be surprised?

I lie in the snow and
Move so carefully.
And when I get up, there's
An angel to see.

With red cheeks and cold toes,
It's time to go in.
I'll warm up a little,
And go out again!

The Sounds of Winter

Woosh, whoosh, blow the winds when a winter storm begins.
(Make the sound of strong, blowing winds.)
Splash, splash says the rain beating on the window pane.
(Make the sound of heavy rain.)
Tip, tip, tap is the sound of ice falling all around.
(Make the sound of an ice storm.)
Suddenly, there's no sound at all as snowflakes start to softly fall.
(Put finger up to lips and say "Shh.")
It snows all night; then *scrape, scrip, scrup!* The noisy snow plow wakes me up!
(Make the sound of a snowplow scraping the street.)
Cheep, chirp, chirp—birds on the snow wait for seeds I throw.
(Make bird sounds.)
"*Woof, woof, woof,* I want to go," says my dog, "and run in the snow!"
(Bark like a dog.)
Ring, ring, the phone rings out. "No school today!" my best friend shouts.
(Make the sound of a phone ringing.)
I put on my coat and shout *"Hooray!"* Then run outside so I can play.
(Shout "Hooray!")

Peanut Butter Snowballs

You Will Need

- 1 small jar of peanut butter
- dry powdered milk
- honey
- flaked coconut

Empty the jar of peanut butter into a bowl. Add 1 to 2 tablespoons of honey (depending on how sweet you want the dough). Stir in 1/4 cup of dry milk. Keep adding small amounts of dry milk until the peanut butter mixture has the consistency of playdough. Invite children to roll the dough into small balls. Next, roll the balls in flaked coconut to make "snowballs." Children can put several together to make a snowman.

Banana Snowman

Place three round slices of banana on top of a lettuce leaf to form a snowman on a plate. Use a pecan half for his hat and raisins for the eyes, nose and mouth. Sprinkle with coconut for snow.

Marshmallow Snowman

Give each student three marshmallows and a toothpick. Let them construct snowmen by sticking the toothpick through the marshmallows. Add raisins, candy sprinkles, or mini chocolate chips for facial features and buttons. Pretzel sticks make great arms. Use a chocolate cookie and chocolate kiss for a hat. Frosting can be used instead of a toothpick to hold the snowmen together.

⚠ Make sure you are aware of any food allergies or restrictions children may have. Be sure children wash their hands before they eat.

Mexican Snowflake

You Will Need

- one package of small flour tortillas
- shredded white cheese such as mozarella, monterey jack or white cheddar

Fold a tortilla in half, then in half again. Cut out shapes and designs with kitchen scissors. Be sure to cut through all the layers, but not across the folds. Carefully open the tortilla and place it flat on a baking sheet. Sprinkle a little cheese on the tortilla and place the baking sheet in a toaster oven or under the broiler for one minute while the cheese melts. Watch carefully. This makes a fun lunch or snack. If you do not have a kitchen or heating appliances, spread peanut butter or jam on the snowflake tortillas.

Hot White Winter Cocoa

You Will Need

- 2 ounces white chocolate baking squares
- 3 cups milk
- 2 cups water
- peppermint stick (optional)

In a double-boiler over medium heat, heat 2 cups of water. In the top saucepan, heat 2 ounces of white baking chocolate. Stir constantly. When the chocolate is melted, bring to a boil and simmer. Add 3 cups of milk and heat until warm. Remove from heat and beat with a whisk until frothy. Ladle into cups and garnish with shavings of white chocolate and a peppermint stick. Serves 6.

Trees in the Snow

You Will Need

- broccoli florets (they look like green trees)
- cauliflower florets (trees/bushes with snow)
- 1/2 cup cottage cheese
- Italian dressing

Place a mound of cottage cheese in a small dish or bowl. Arrange the florets in the cottage cheese as if they were trees in the snow. Drizzle a little Italian dressing to flavor the snack.

When it's
cold outside,
you must
dress warmly.
Draw a
hat and mittens
on this boy.

1

Snowflakes are all different.
Color your favorite snowflake.
2
It is fun to build snowmen.
Can you draw the arms on these three?
3

Polar bears love the cold.
Draw a yummy snack for them.
4
Playing outside
in winter is fun!
5

Name

Warm Up with Some Math

Complete the math problems.
Then match the letters with the correct numbers at the bottom of the page.
Write the letters on the lines. If you have young children, do this as a class.

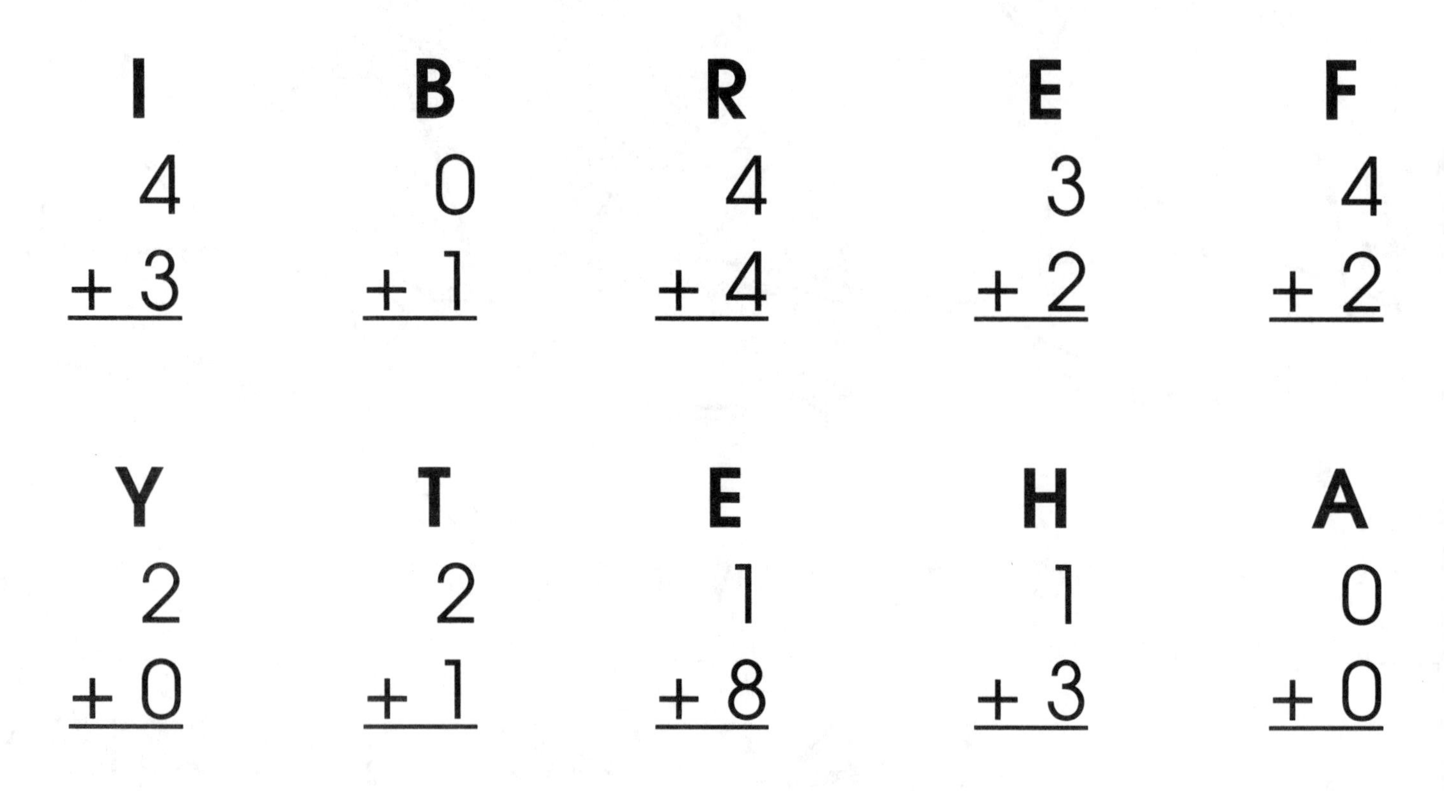

I	B	R	E	F
4	0	4	3	4
+ 3	+ 1	+ 4	+ 2	+ 2

Y	T	E	H	A
2	2	1	1	0
+ 0	+ 1	+ 8	+ 3	+ 0

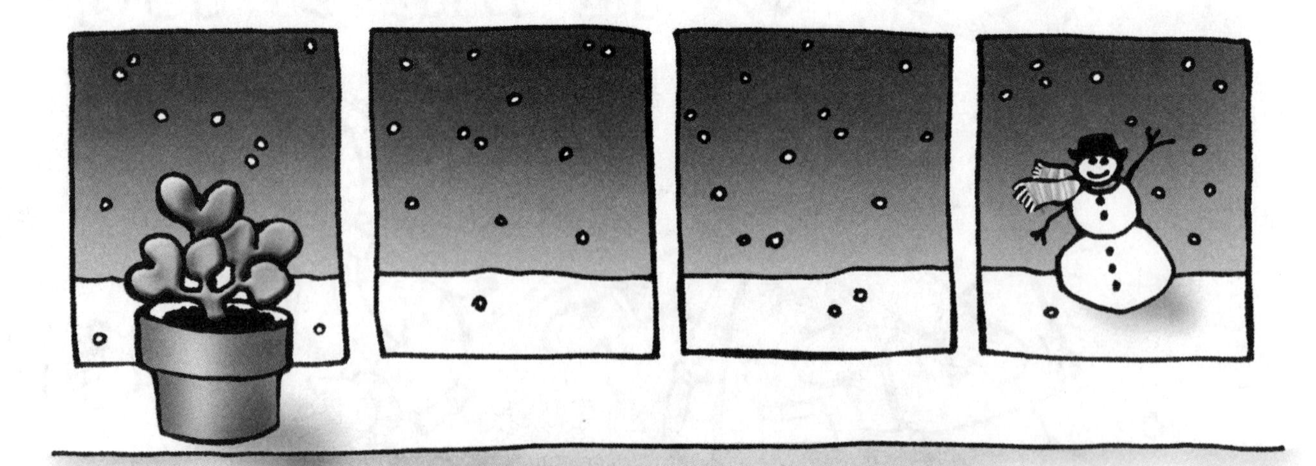

When it's cold outside, where is the best place to be?

___ ___   ___ ___ ___   ___ ___ ___ ___
1 2   3 4 5   6 7 8 9

Name

Dress Warmly!

Draw a line from each picture to its name.

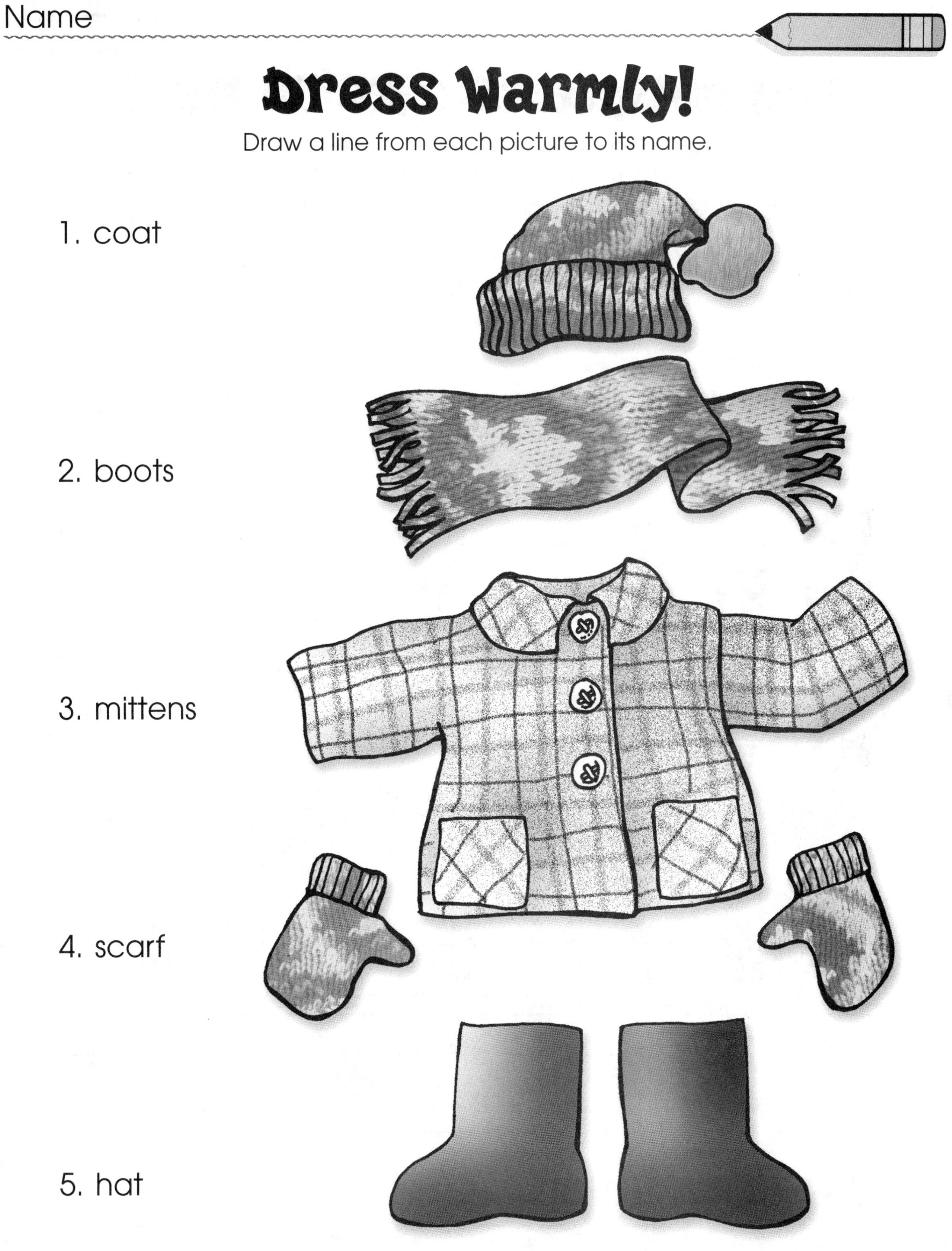

1. coat
2. boots
3. mittens
4. scarf
5. hat

Name

Snowflake Patterns

Write the letter of the snowflake that should appear next in the pattern.

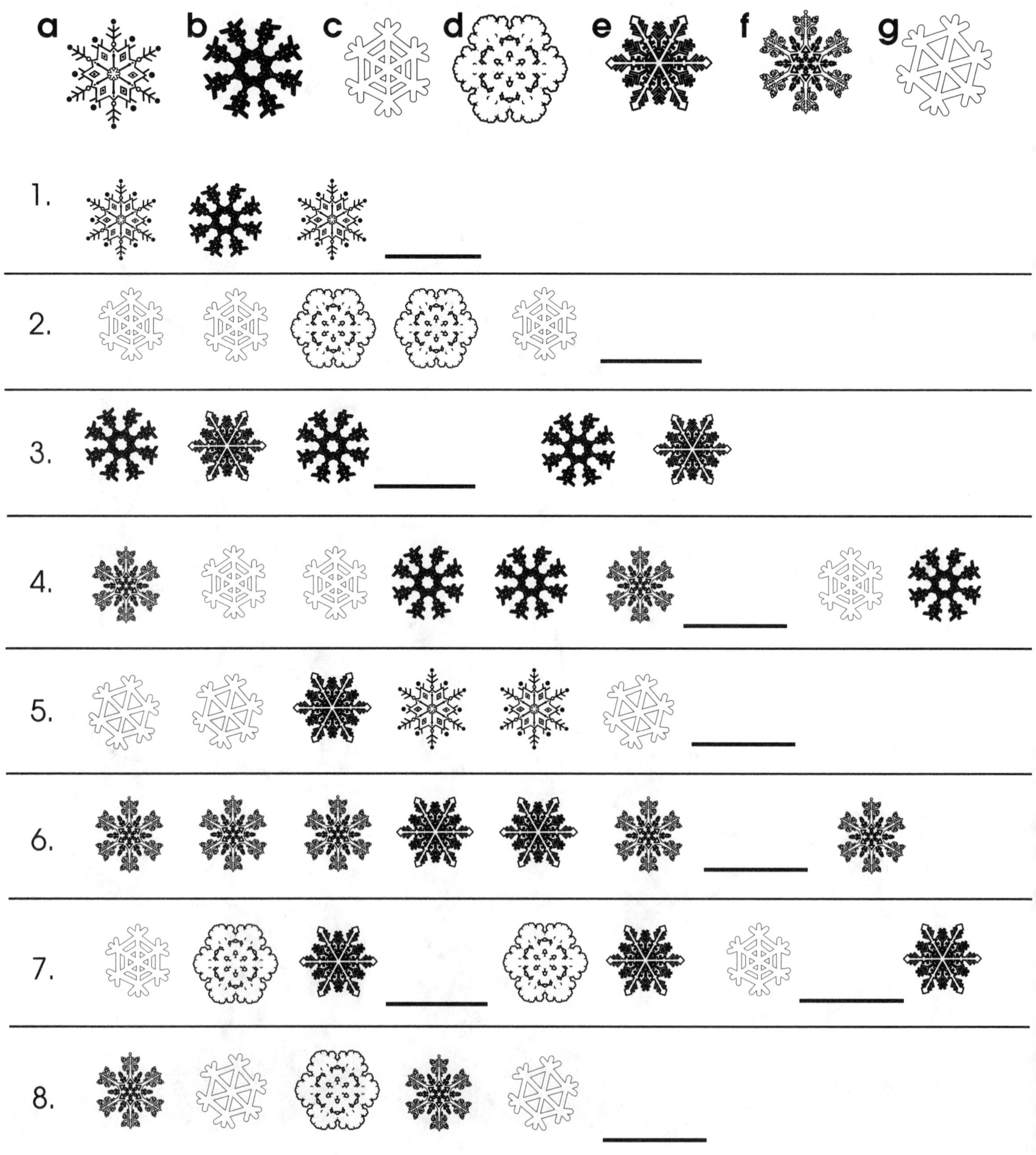

Name

Winter Acrostic

Use the letters in the word *winter* to write words about winter.
(Example: w—wool socks)

Name
Snowflake Counting
Count the snowflakes, then write the correct number of snoflakes on the line.
1. ____
2. ____
3. ____
4. ____
5. ____

Name ______________________________

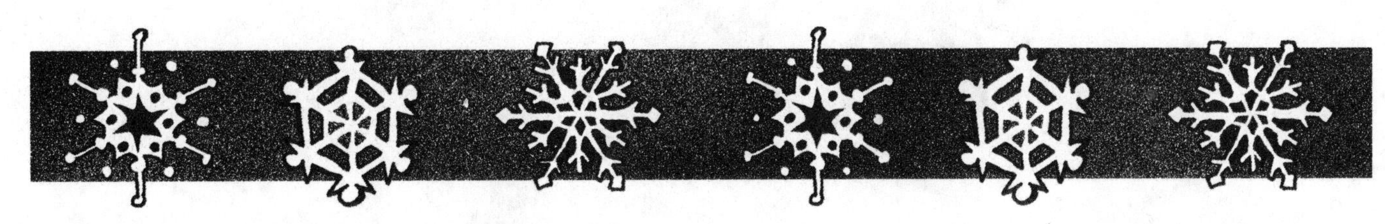

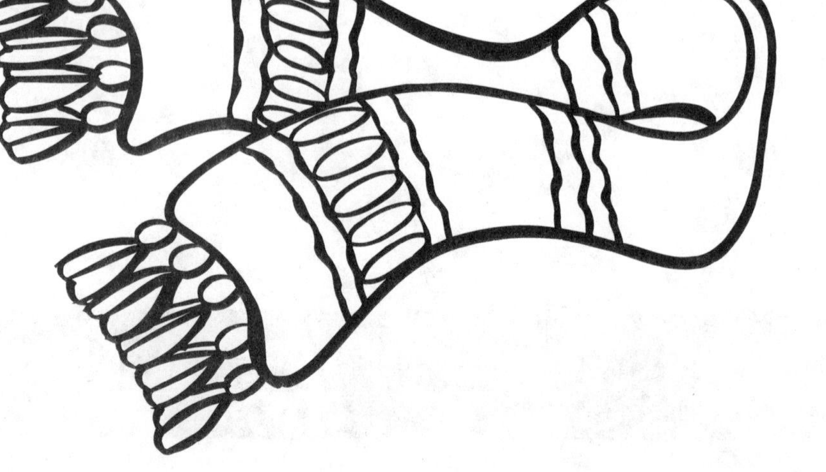

Book Cover

Name ___________________________

Winter Poster to Color

Christmas Stockings

Reproduce the stocking pattern on page 86, one per child. Cut it out and allow each child to decorate a stocking. Write, or have children write, their names at the top of the stockings. Use these stockings to complete the bulletin board on page 85.

Christmas Cookie Ornaments

Bring a variety of Christmas cookie cutters and modeling clay. Help children roll out the clay and cut out one to two Christmas shapes. Poke a small hole at the top of each shape. Allow to dry overnight. Let children use paints to decorate their ornaments.

Share the Holiday Spirit

Reproduce clip art on pages 101-102. Fold colored construction paper in half to create Christmas cards. Have children color the clip art images and glue them to the fronts of the cards to create holiday pictures. Help children write *Happy Holidays* or *Merry Christmas* inside. Take the cards to a local hospital or senior center to spread some holiday cheer.

Bulletin Board

1. Cover a bulletin board with red and green paper, alternating colors.
2. Use string to hang the decorated stockings from the activity on page 84. Make sure each child has a stocking. Create two to three rows of stockings.
3. Put the title *Merry Christmas* across the top.

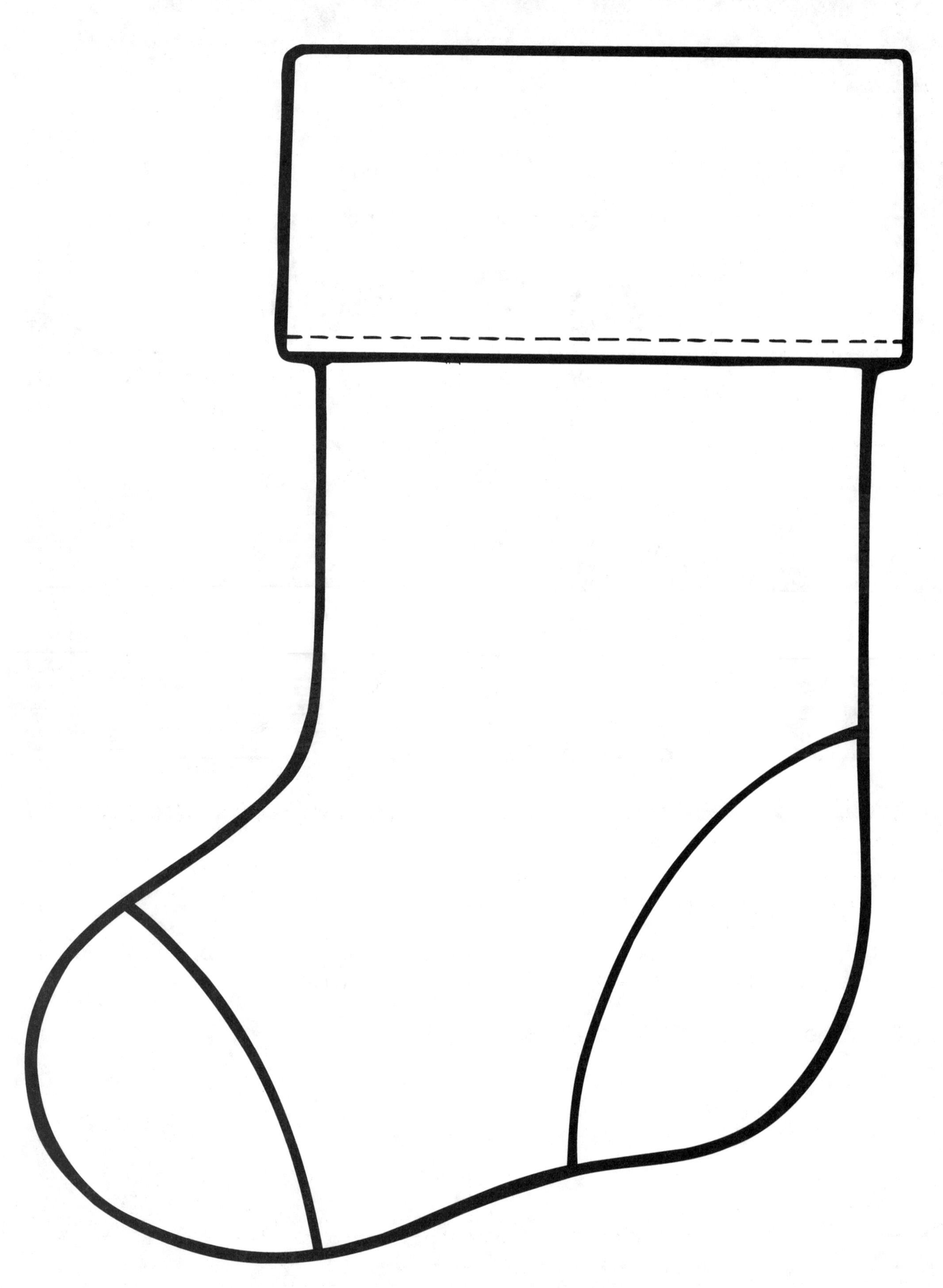

Books

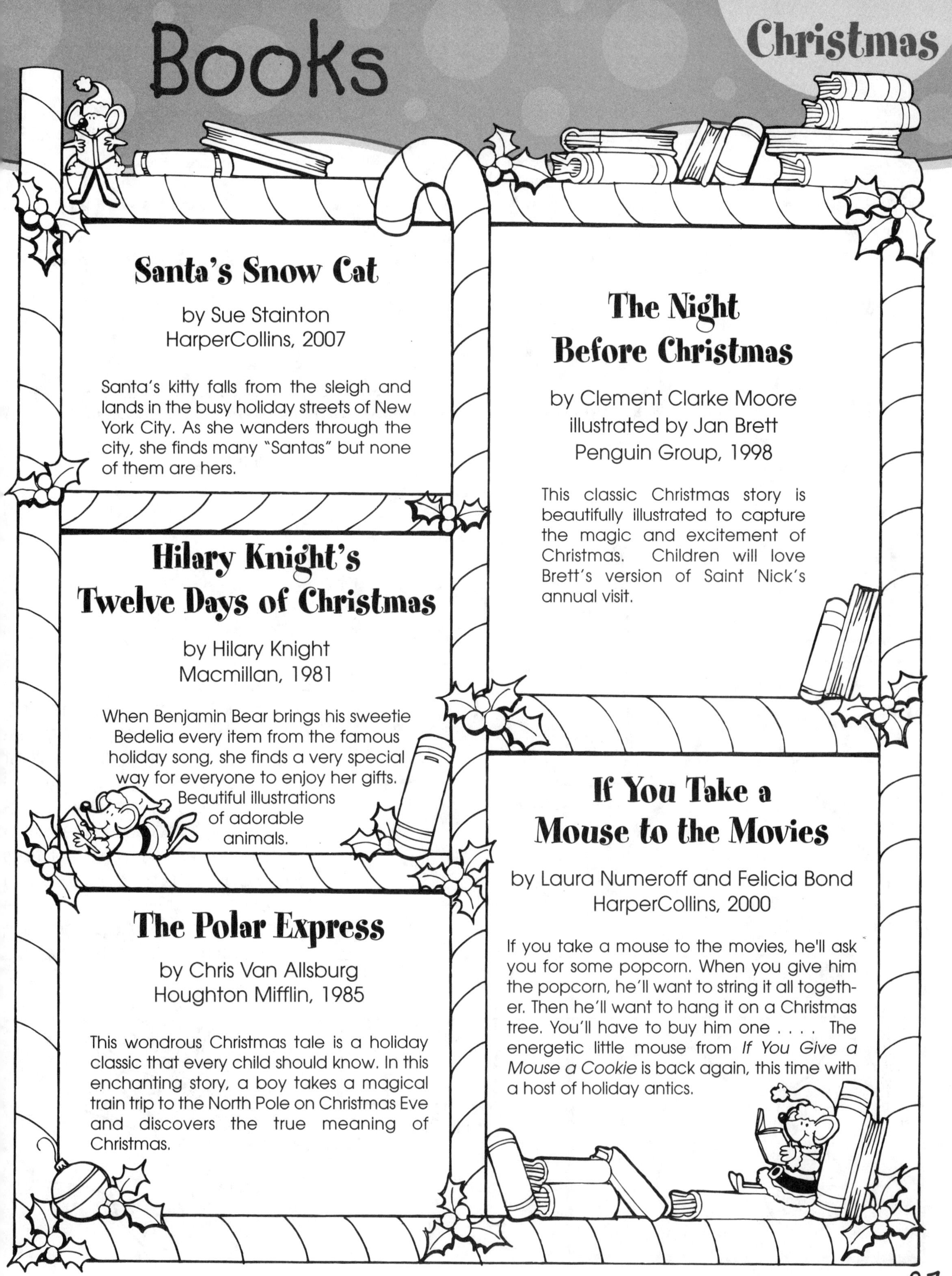

Santa's Snow Cat

by Sue Stainton
HarperCollins, 2007

Santa's kitty falls from the sleigh and lands in the busy holiday streets of New York City. As she wanders through the city, she finds many "Santas" but none of them are hers.

Hilary Knight's Twelve Days of Christmas

by Hilary Knight
Macmillan, 1981

When Benjamin Bear brings his sweetie Bedelia every item from the famous holiday song, she finds a very special way for everyone to enjoy her gifts. Beautiful illustrations of adorable animals.

The Polar Express

by Chris Van Allsburg
Houghton Mifflin, 1985

This wondrous Christmas tale is a holiday classic that every child should know. In this enchanting story, a boy takes a magical train trip to the North Pole on Christmas Eve and discovers the true meaning of Christmas.

The Night Before Christmas

by Clement Clarke Moore
illustrated by Jan Brett
Penguin Group, 1998

This classic Christmas story is beautifully illustrated to capture the magic and excitement of Christmas. Children will love Brett's version of Saint Nick's annual visit.

If You Take a Mouse to the Movies

by Laura Numeroff and Felicia Bond
HarperCollins, 2000

If you take a mouse to the movies, he'll ask you for some popcorn. When you give him the popcorn, he'll want to string it all together. Then he'll want to hang it on a Christmas tree. You'll have to buy him one . . . . The energetic little mouse from *If You Give a Mouse a Cookie* is back again, this time with a host of holiday antics.

Prancing Reindeer and Busy Elves

You Will Need

scissors
glue
yarn
pom-poms
craft eyes
construction paper
lightweight cardboard

Directions

Reproduce and cut out the patterns to the left. Enlarge if necessary. Glue them to lightweight cardboard. Then, cut out the finger holes. Color the body patterns. Glue on craft eyes and pom-pom noses. Cut antlers and ears from construction paper and glue them to the reindeer pattern. Add yarn hair and hat trim to the elf pattern.

Reindeer Example

Reindeer Patterns

Elf Example

Elf Pattern

Holiday Gift Certificates and Holder

You Will Need

- white paper
- pencils
- crayons
- glue
- holiday stickers
- colored paper
- markers
- ruler
- tape

Directions

1. Cut out several 5" x 3" pieces of white paper for certificates.
2. Have each child fill in several certificates and draw a picture or glue a cutout picture on each. Or you may want to let them choose from cards you've already written.
3. They should sign their name to each one.
4. For the holder, cut a 7" x 6" piece of colored paper.
5. Fold the bottom up 3".
6. Glue or tape the sides.
7. Put the gift certificates inside the holder.
8. Fold the top down and decorate with markers and holiday stickers.
9. Have them write the name of the person they're giving the certificates to on the holder.

Santa Is Watching

You Will Need

red pom-poms
glue
scissors
two 2" x 2" squares of heavy paper
cotton balls
crayons

Directions

1. Color and cut out the pattern pieces on page 91.
2. Cut along the broken lines of the eyes on Santa's face.
3. Glue cotton balls to the round pattern for the hat.
4. Fold the hat over as shown in the sketch below.
5. Glue the cotton-covered piece to the point on Santa's hat.
6. Glue the holly leaves on the hat. Add red pom-poms on the holly for berries.
7. Insert the eye strip into eye slits.
8. Fold the 2" x 2" paper squares in half.
9. Glue the folded paper squares to the ends of the eye strip. This will keep the eye strip from sliding out.

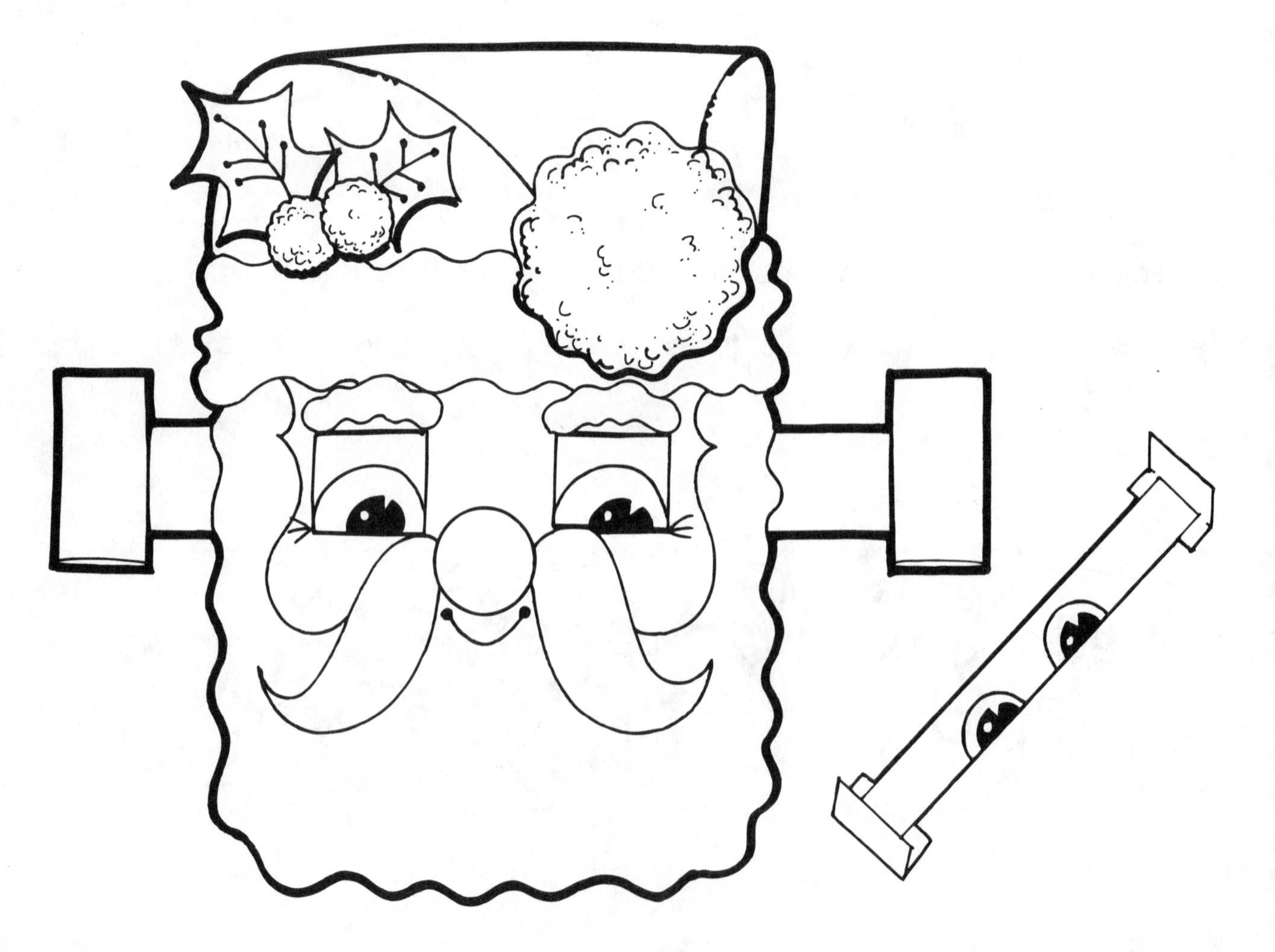

Santa Is Watching Patterns

Christmas Sounds

ACTION RHYME

Christmas is filled with happy sounds.
You can hear them all around.
Christmas carols fill the air;
Voices singing everywhere!
(Sing: "Deck the halls with boughs of holly. Fa-la-la-la-la, la-la-la-la!")
Bells are ringing, jingling too,
Bringing merry thoughts to you.
(Sing: "Jingle bells, jingle bells, jingle all the way!")
The stores are filled with happy crowds
And jolly Santa laughs out loud.
(Say: "Ho, ho, ho" and hold your stomach!)
In the yards and on the roofs
Reindeer dance with clicking hooves.
(Make clip, clop noises with your tongue and run in place.)
You can see the pretty lights
Twinkling on the trees tonight!
(Say: "Twinkle, twinkle" and flash your fingers like lights.)
In the windows of the stores
Drummer boys beat drums galore.
(Say: "Prum, prum, prum, prum" as you pretend to beat a drum!)
People all around you say,
"Have a happy holiday!"
*(Sing: "We wish you a Merry Christmas, we wish you a Merry Christmas,
we wish you a Merry Christmas, and a Happy New Year!")*

Chinese Nutty Clusters

You Will Need

12 oz. chocolate chips
12 oz. butterscotch chips
1 oz. square of unsweetened chocolate
$^{1}/_{2}$ cup peanuts
6 oz. of crispy Chinese noodles

Melt the chips and chocolate square in the microwave or over low heat on the stove. Once melted, add the peanuts and noodles. Mix well. Drop by teaspoons on waxed paper. Let cool and harden. These treats can be placed in clear plastic-containers and decorated with holiday stickers and ribbon.

Holiday Yummies

You Will Need

small bowknot pretzels
Hershey's kisses®
m & m's®

Remove wrappers from kisses. Place the pretzels on a baking sheet. Place a kiss on top of each pretzel. Bake for 2 minutes in a preheated 350°F oven. Top each treat with an m & m. Let harden (place in freezer if children are really anxious!). These treats are not only yummy, but colorful too!

Reindeer Cookies

You Will Need

heart-shaped sugar cookies
chocolate chips
small pretzel sticks
chocolate frosting
red m & m's®

Bake heart-shaped cookies. Frost. Break pretzel sticks to look like antlers. Use chocolate chips for eyes and a red m&m for the nose. Enjoy!

⚠ Make sure you are aware of any food allergies or restrictions children may have. Be sure children wash their hands before they eat.

This card colored with love by

Name

De-Lightful Words

Identify the Christmas word on each strand of lights.

Name
Santa's Colorful Helpers
Help Santa's helpers color the ribbons the correct color.
red
blue
brown
green
yellow
purple

Name

Busy Elf Match

Cut and paste the lowercase letter next to the matching capital letter.

Name

Christmas Rebus

Color the pictures below. Cut out the pictures and paste each one in the story where you think it makes the most sense. Then read your story to someone at home.

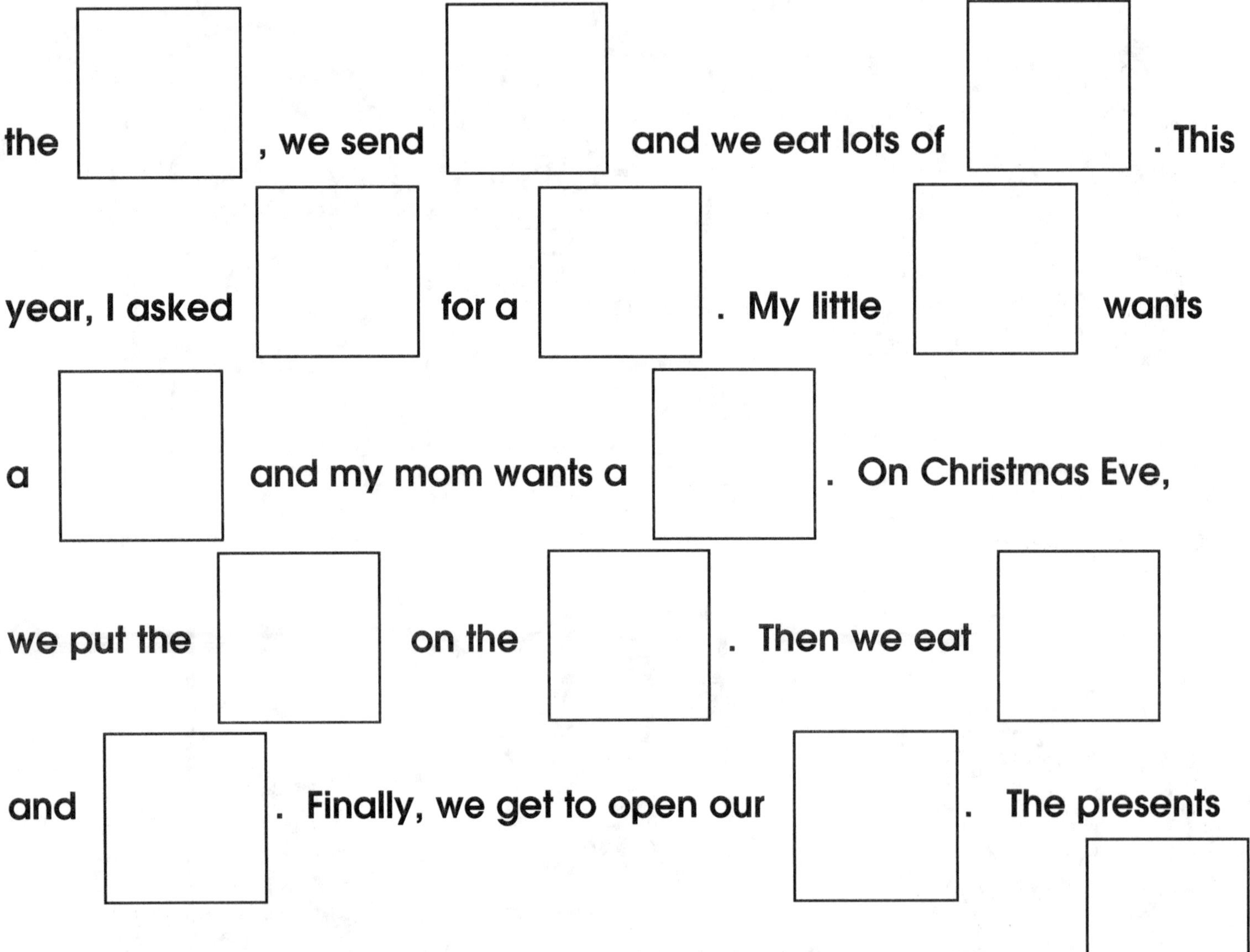

I love Christmas because we do so many fun things. We decorate the ____, we send ____ and we eat lots of ____. This year, I asked ____ for a ____. My little ____ wants a ____ and my mom wants a ____. On Christmas Eve, we put the ____ on the ____. Then we eat ____ and ____. Finally, we get to open our ____. The presents are nice, but the best thing about Christmas is being with my ____.

Name

Striped Stocking

Draw and color the correct number of stripes on each stocking.

Name
My
Christmas
Page

Merry
Christmas

Clip Art

Merry
Christmas

Book Cover

Name ______________________________

Christmas Poster to Color

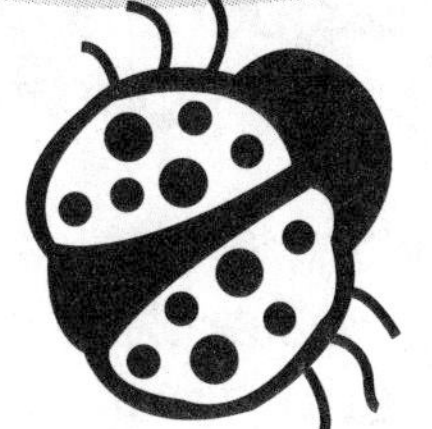

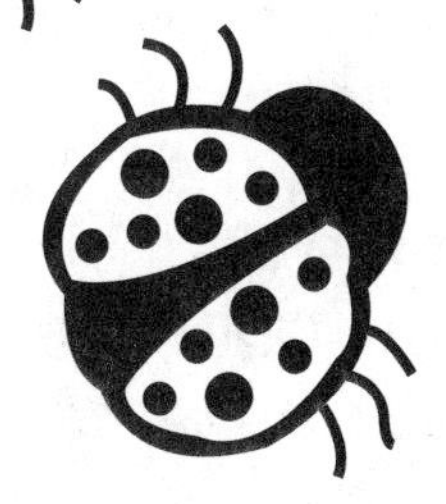

How Flowers Drink

You Will Need

white or light yellow flower such as a daffodil or tulip
clear glass of water
red or blue food coloring

Directions

1. Mix food coloring with the water to make a bright color.
2. Cut 1/2" off the bottom of the flower stem.
3. Put the flower stem in the water.
4. Watch the flower over the next few hours to see the flower turn the color of the water.
5. Talk about how a flower uses its stem to "drink" water from the ground.

Shadow Tag

On a warm, sunny day, have children play a game of shadow tag. Designate one player to be "it." Have him or her chase the others and instead of tagging another person, "it" must touch the other person's shadow with his or her own shadow. When a shadow is tagged, that player becomes "it." The game continues until all children have had a turn.

A Buggy Study

Take children for a walk outside on a sunny day to look for harmless bugs such as black ants, ladybugs, grasshoppers, caterpillars, and the praying mantis. Take along jars with holes punched in the lids or zip-up plastic bags with holes punched in them to collect the bugs you find. Put each bug in a container of its own.

When you return from the walk, set the jars on a table so children can look at the bugs. (If you put the bugs in plastic bags, transfer them to jars.) Talk about the bugs.

- How are the bugs the same and how are they different?
- How many legs does each bug have?
- Do any of them have wings?
- How do the bugs compare in size?

Look up each bug in an insect guide to find out what it eats, where it lives, and if it is harmful or helpful to farmers and gardeners.

Have each child draw a picture of his or her favorite bug and give it a pet name.

When the study is over, release the bugs back into their natural habitat.

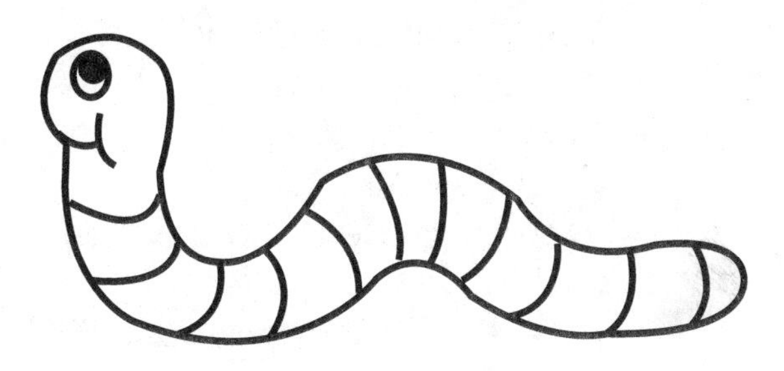

Spring or Summer Nature Hike

Summer is a wonderful time for students to observe nature. Give each child a zipper bag to collect and display their findings.

- Write the child's name on each bag.
- Display these bags on a bulletin board. Be sure not to zip the bags tight if they contain things that might mold.

Seed Graphing

Collect a variety of seeds from things such as pumpkins, sunflowers, peas, corn and squash. Give each child a handful of seeds and a copy of the seed chart on page 107. Have them glue the seeds on the chart or they can draw pictures of the seeds if they wish. You may need to write the names of the seeds on the chart for the children.

A Taste of Summer

When vegetable gardens are at their peak in mid to late summer, bring fresh produce for children to explore. On a table, lay out fresh vegetables such as peas, carrots, corn, beans, cucumbers, zucchini, tomatoes, radishes, etc. Have children examine the vegetables. Ask questions about each one, such as:

- What color is it?
- Is it small, medium or large?
- Does it have a thick or thin skin?
- What shape is it?
- Does it smell good or bad?

Have children decide which is the smallest, the largest, the hardest, the softest and the longest.

Cut each vegetable in half and have children look at and touch the insides. Discuss the seeds of the tomato and cucumber. Talk about which vegetables grow on top of the ground and which ones grow underground.

Finally, cut a small piece of each vegetable for the children to taste. Let them vote on which tastes best. Discuss different ways these vegetables are eaten.

Name ______________

My Seed Chart

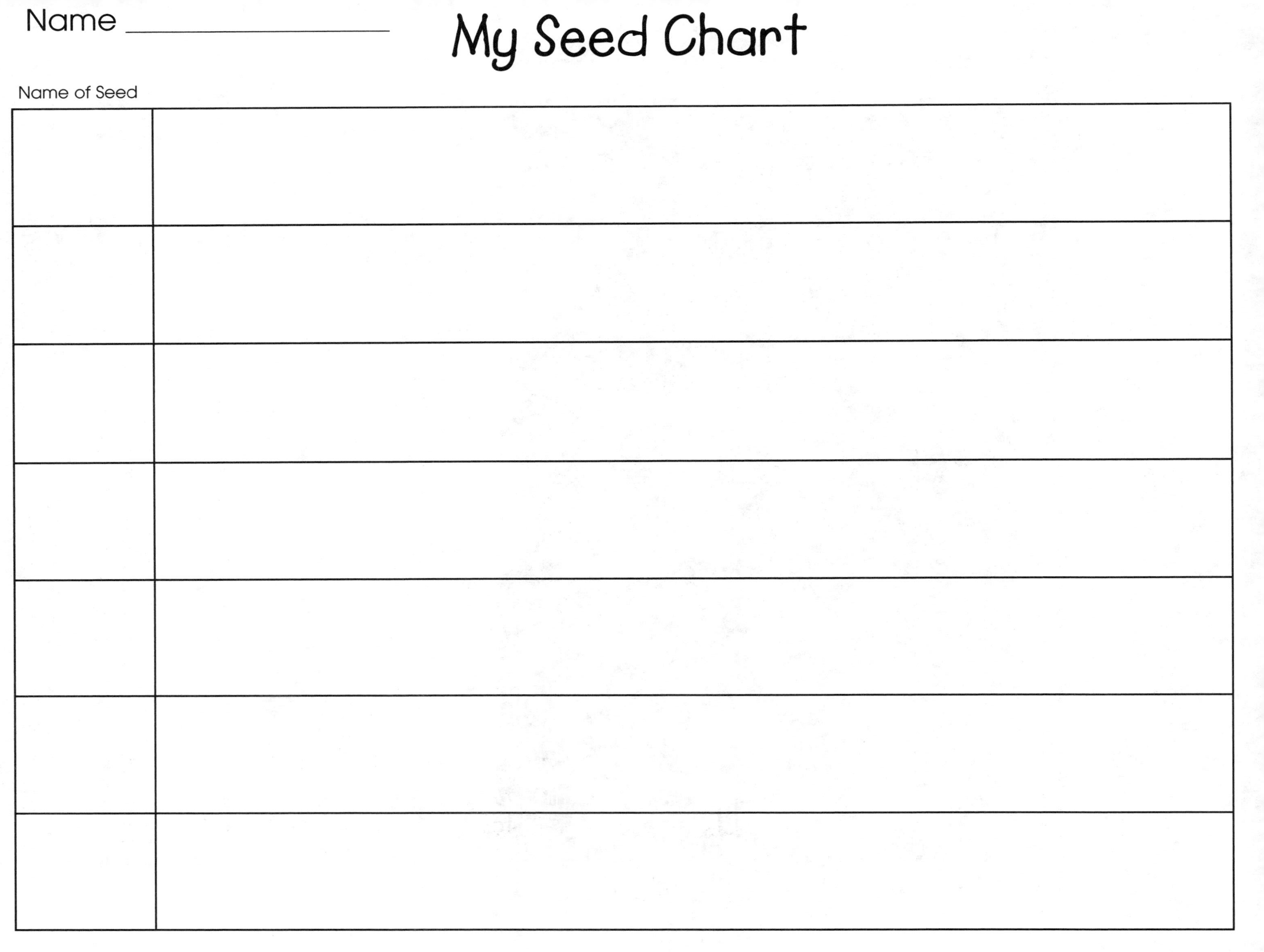

Name of Seed	

Wish Upon a Star Bulletin Board

1. Cover the bulletin board with dark blue paper.
2. Using colored construction paper, cut out the letters for the title "Wish Upon a Star."
3. Cut out stars from yellow construction paper.
4. Allow children to choose stars and write their names on them.
5. Attach the stars to the board.

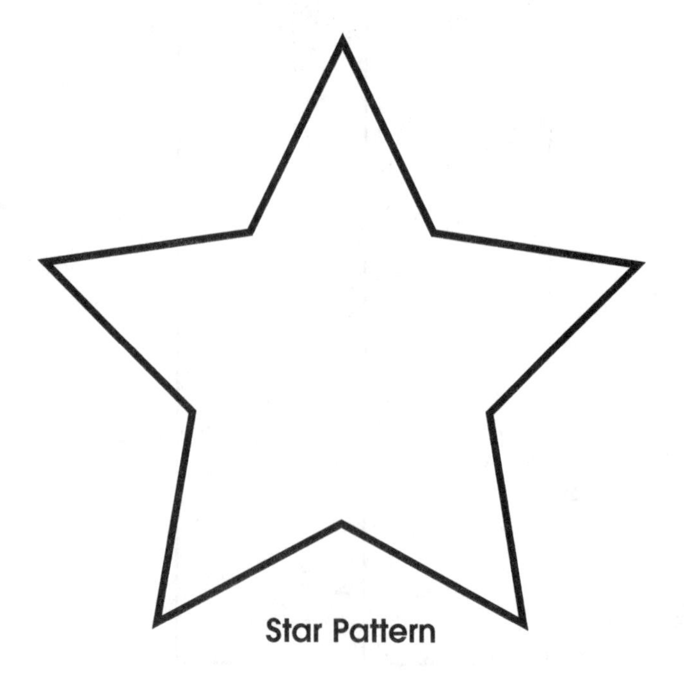

Star Pattern

The Search for Spring

by Else Holmelund Minarik, HarperFestival, 2002

After a long cold winter, Little Bear is ready for spring, but when will it arrive? With help from a grumpy groundhog, Little Bear and his friends help get spring started.

When Will It Be Spring?

by Catherine Walters, Dutton Books, 2001

This is the charming story of Alfie the Bear who is too excited to sleep during the winter. He's so excited that he keeps waking his mother up to see if spring has come. His mother gives him things to watch for, but Alfie mistakes snowflakes for white butterflies. A wonderful book!

Hopper Hunts for Spring

by Marcus Pfister, North South Books, 1995

When looking for spring, Hopper encounters some wonderful new animal friends. A delightful book with excellent watercolor pictures.

Spring

by Ron Hirschi and Thomas D. Magelsen (Photographer)
Scott Foresman, 1996

The wonders of the natural world come alive after a long, cold winter. Gorgeous photos of sprouting flowers, nesting birds, and melting snow make this a must-have for your library.

Spring Song

by Barbara Sculing, Gulliver Books, 2001

The author asks readers to predict how various animals and people will react to the coming of spring. The answers are written in rhyme and the illustrations are colorful.

Watermelon Magnets

Summer is the time for watermelons. Start with one green and one pink foam sheet (found at craft stores). Have the children cut a large half circle from the green. They should then cut a smaller half circle from the pink. Glue the smaller section to the larger green section as shown. Glue real watermelon seeds to the foam and place a magnetic strip on the back.

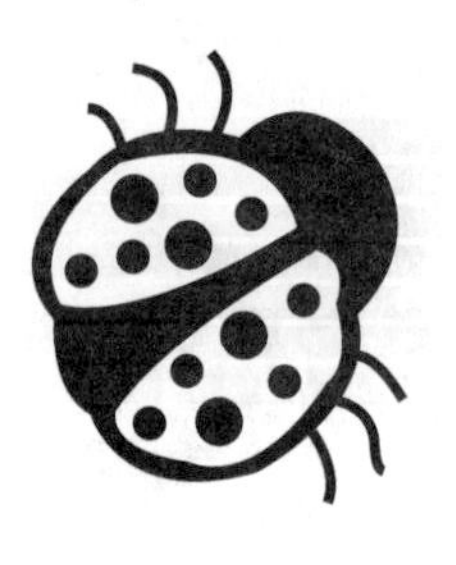

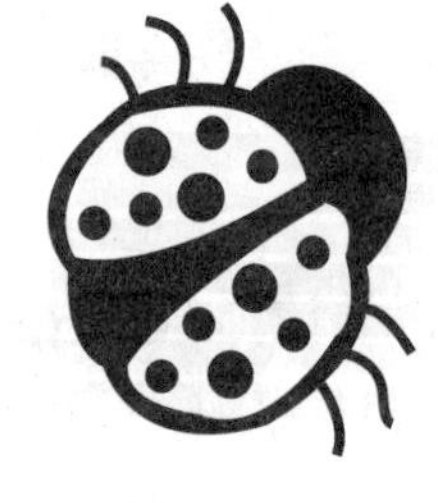

Ladybugs

Have enough walnut shells for each child to have a half shell. Paint the walnut shell red and allow to dry. With a cotton swab dipped in black paint or with a black marker, add dots.

Variation: Smooth rocks can be used. Have the children give them as paperweight gifts.

Thumbprint Spiders

Children can make their own spiders just by using their fingerprints. Help children dip their thumbs into black paint and then press their thumbprint onto a piece of white paper. Do the same thing with another finger to form the head of the spider. Children can then draw the eight legs with a fine-tip marker.

Sparkly Webs

On a dark piece of construction paper, draw a spiderweb with a marker. Make one for each child. Have children squeeze white glue over the lines of the web. Then sprinkle with glitter and allow the glue to dry.

Spring
POEM

Rainy Days

Don't you love a rainy day, especially in the spring?
Drip, drop! Plip, plop! It waters everything.

The flowers drink it up and bloom before your eyes.
The squirrel's tail shields him from the rain as he eats his acorn prize.

Robins hop around the yard with eyes to the ground.
They know that on rainy days fat worms can be found!

I love to smell the clean scent that spring rains give the air.
And sometimes there's a rainbow to make me stop and stare.

And when the rain is over, I'm outside in a flash!
I'm wearing my boots and am ready to splash!

Activity
Have children draw pictures to illustrate the poem. Then use watercolor paints to add the raindrops.

Ask children to share their favorite things to do on rainy days.

Snacks

Trail Mix

Have the children mix these ingredients together and put in individual bags. This is a great snack for students to take on a hike around the neighborhood.

Goldfish® crackers
m & m's®
Cheerios® cereal
pretzel sticks
peanuts
raisins

Smiles

You will need: red apples, peanut butter, mini-marshmallows

Cut apples into wedges and smear peanut butter on one side. Place mini-marshmallows in the peanut butter and place another wedge on top. The red skin of the apple resembles lips and the mini-marshmallows are teeth!

Spider Crackers

Using two round crackers, make a peanut butter sandwich. Insert eight pretzel sticks into the sandwich. Use peanut butter to attach m & m eyes.

Snack Crackers

You Will Need

2 large bags of oyster crackers
3/4 cup oil
1/4 tsp. garlic powder
1/4 tsp. lemon pepper
1/2 tsp. dill weed
1 pkg. Hidden Valley Ranch Dressing®

Mix all ingredients except crackers in large zip-type bag. Add crackers and shake well.

Optional: Bake in 250°F oven for 15-20 minutes. Cool and serve.

Sand Buckets

Crush graham crackers or vanilla sandwich cookies and sprinkle them on top of vanilla pudding mixture to resemble sand. You can hide gummy worms in the sand.

Optional: Make these in mini sand buckets and place paper umbrellas in the buckets.

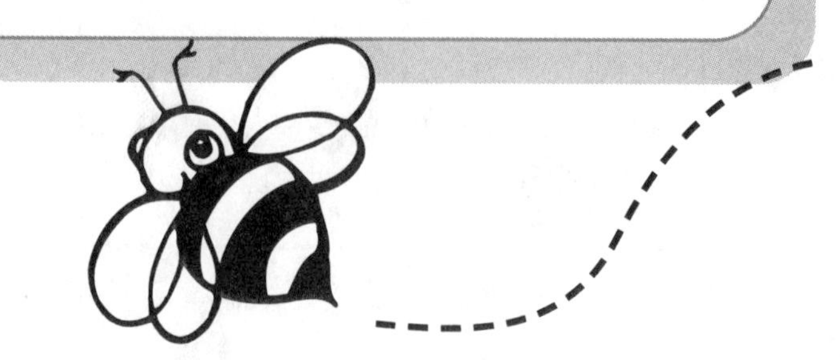

⚠ Make sure you are aware of any food allergies or restrictions children may have.
Be sure children wash their hands before they eat.

My Book of Summer Colors

Name

Summer colors are great!

Color these summer objects.

Summer flowers are color showers!

Color the flowers red and yellow.

2

Watermelons are pink on the inside.

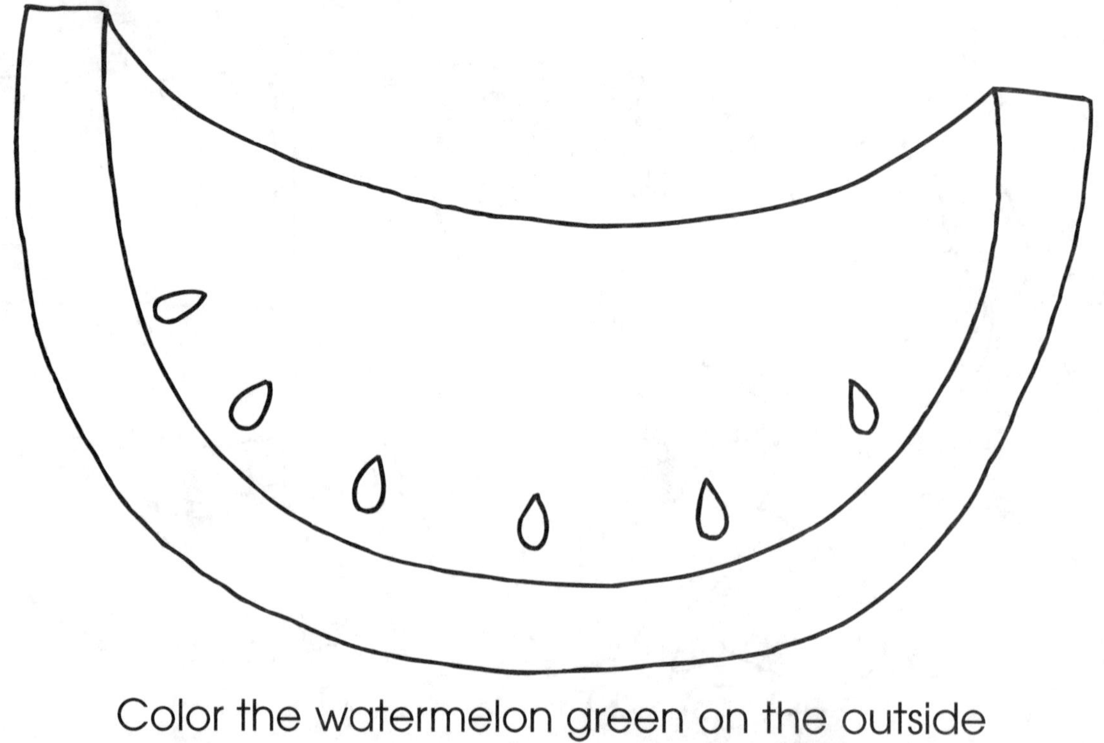

Color the watermelon green on the outside and pink on the inside with black seeds.

3

Tomatoes make a yummy, red treat!

Color the tomatoes red and the stems green.

4

Birds fly high in the sky!

Color the birds blue, red and yellow.

5

The grass is as green as I've ever seen.

Color the grass different shades of green.

6

The bright yellow sun shines on everyone.

Color the sun yellow.

7

Name

Beginning Sounds

Circle the letter that shows the beginning sound for each picture.

Name

Squirmy Worms

Fill in the letters that are missing on each worm.

Name

Spring Maze

Help the bee find his way to the flowers.

Name

Write the Number

How many objects are in each set? Write the number.

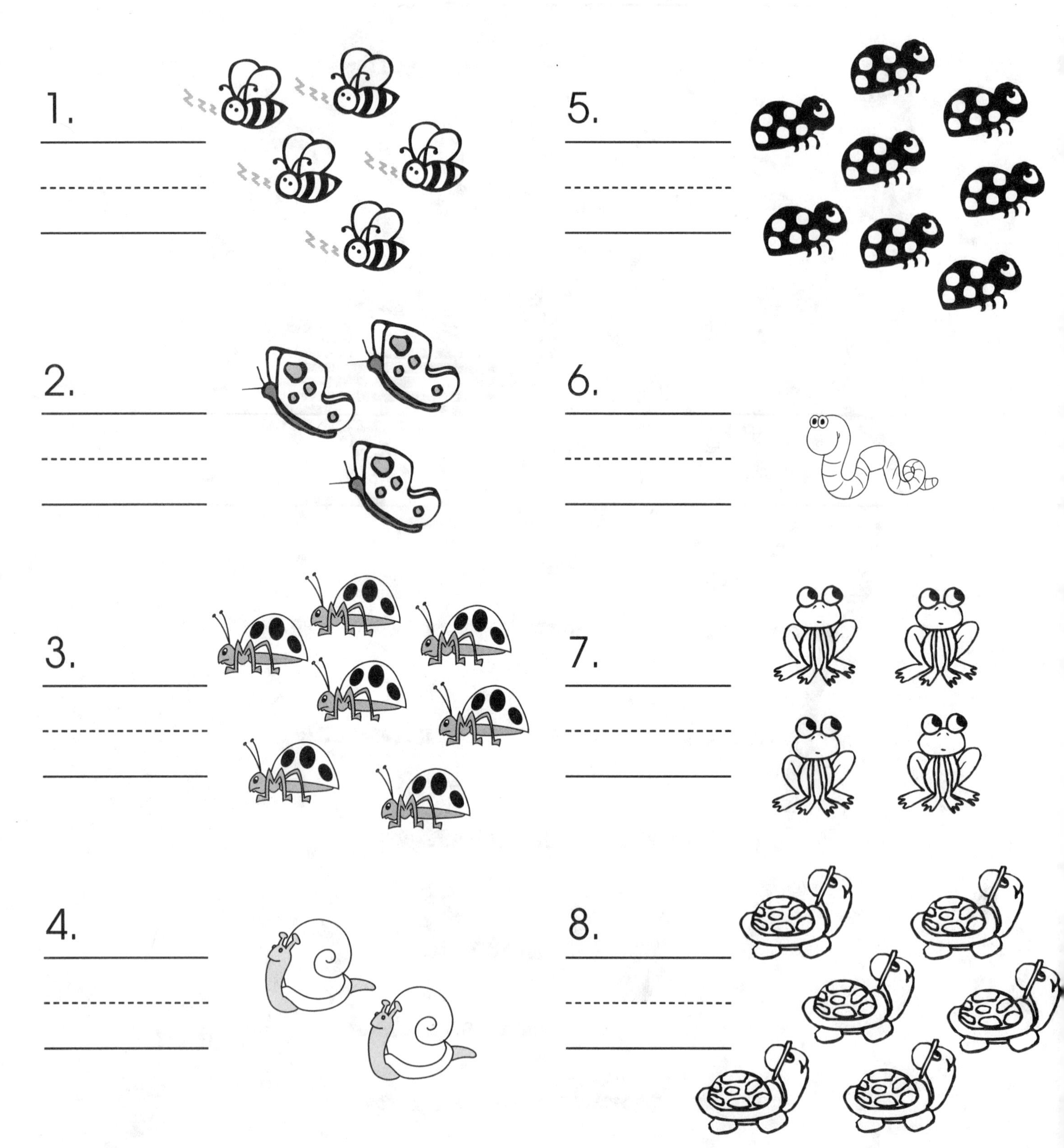

Name

Flowers for Mom

Count the flowers in each bouquet.
Then write the number on the vase.

Name

Let's Count to 100!

Write the missing numbers to count from 1 to 100.

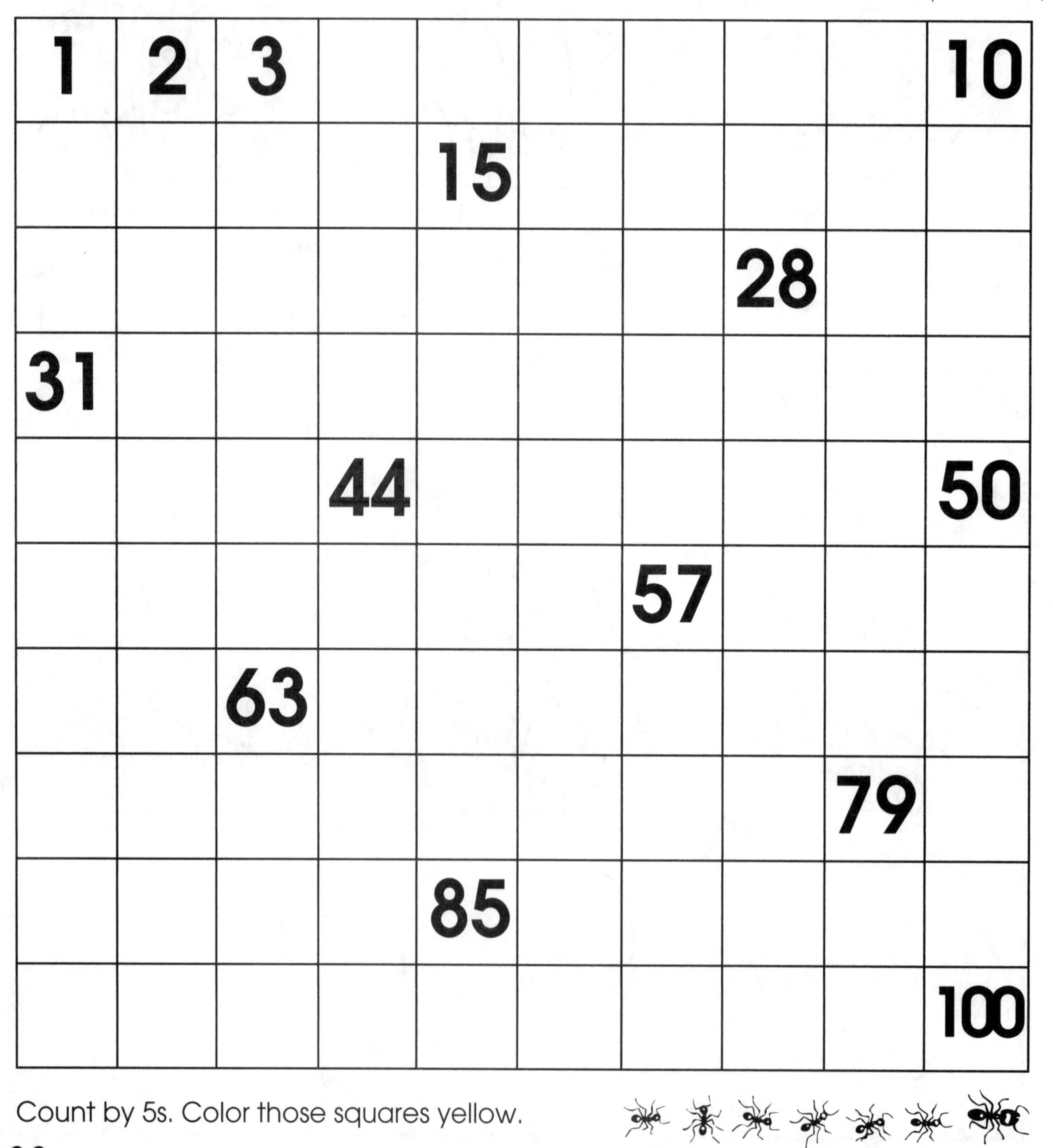

1	2	3							10
				15					
							28		
31									
			44						50
						57			
		63							
								79	
				85					
									100

Count by 5s. Color those squares yellow.

Name

Summer Patterns

Look at the pattern in each row. Draw the next object.

Name ______________________________

My Spring and Summer Page

Clip Art

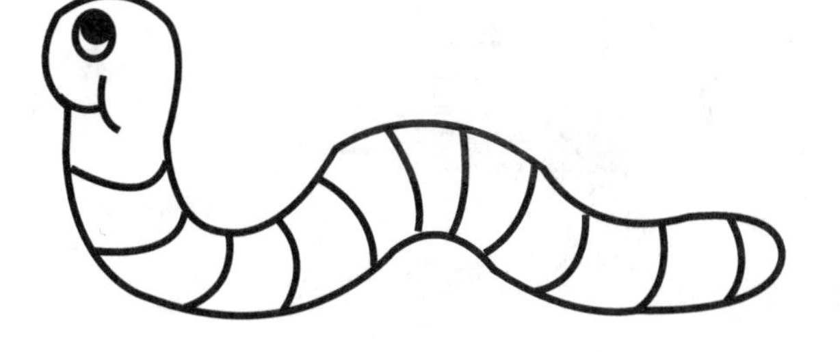

Book Cover

Name ___________________________

Spring and Summer Poster to Color